# Mercy Reigns

## Book 1: The City of Lights

By M. Sue Alexander

This book is a work of fiction.  Names and characters in the story are a product of the author's imagination.  Any resemblance to actual persons, living or dead, events or locales, is coincidental.  Should you purchase a copy of this book without a cover, be aware this book may be stolen property and neither the publisher nor the author has received payment for a "stripped book."

Book 1: The Millennial Reign
**Book 1: Mercy Reigns**
FIRST EDITION 2023, USA
SUZANDER PUBLISHING



**Book Cover by Christine Roszak**

**View M. Sue's Website and Facebook Page
www.msuealexanderbooks.com**

*M. Sue Alexander*

# Series Titles by Author

## Resurrection Dawn 2014 Series

*Book 1: Resurrection Dawn 2014  Book 2: The Christian Fugitive*
*Book 3: Rebels in Paradise  Book 4: Veil of Lies*
*Book 5: The Anointing  Book 6: Countdown to Justice*
*Book 7: All Rise  Book 8: Unlikely Suspect*
*Book 9: Lethal Snapshot  Book 10: Purgatory*
*Book 11: April Fool's Day  Book 12: Reign of Errors*

## Time of Jacob's Trouble

*Book 1: The Four Horsemen  Book 2: Beast*
*Book 3: Witness  Book 4: The Word*
*Book 5: Judgment  Book 6: Deceiver*
*Book 7: False Prophet  Book 8: Satan*
*Book 9: The Image*
*Book 10: Jesus the Appearance*

## Crystal Creek Mysteries

*Book 1: Two Dead on Crystal Creek*
*Book 2: Poison Tea*
*Book 3: A Latte to Die For*
*Book 4: Drop Dead Gorgeous*

## Independent Titles

*Adam's Bones*
*Encounters of the God-Kind*
*Out of Time: The Vanderbilt Incident*
*The Forum*
*The Minister's Haunting*
*Tomorrow's Promise*

# Author's Comments

At the Second Coming of Jesus Christ to earth, He ascends from Heaven with an army of angels, the Twelve Apostles, and a select number of spiritually-transformed humans. The Mount of Olives splits in half from east to west at the moment Jesus' feet touch earth, raising Jerusalem to great heights while valleys to the north and south are formed. He defends Israel during the Battle of Armageddon, then imprisons Satan, the Antichrist, and the False Prophet. They will not be loosed until the end of the Millennium Reign to fight one last battle.

While Jesus, wrapped in God's glory, rules the world from the Jerusalem Temple, people who live beyond the borders of Israel, and survived God's harsh seven-year judgments, dwell in a wilderness. They birth children, grow old, and die. Their souls remain in the grave until Jesus defeats Satan again during a final war and raises them.

Jesus has returned to earth to fulfill Old Testament prophecies scripted by Daniel, Isaiah, Ezekiel, and others. World citizens are required to obey certain new rules. War between nations must cease. Certain animals are no longer enemies. One person from each community is required to visit Jesus once a year or rain will not fall on their land.

As time progresses, people congregate and build back infrastructures while rediscovering the conveniences formerly enjoyed by their ancestors—like electricity, clean-water systems, and communication. Some descendants of Christians choose to forge their own destinies. People must choose to obey and worship Jesus while time exists.

This work of fiction depicts how Cory and Mary Lindsey's descendants during three different time periods displayed their faith in Jesus.

# 167 ASC

# 1

**"AFTER THE SECOND COMING,** one city still stands."

"The City of Lights," I tell my father. "Were there others?'

"Yes, mostly rural towns and farms," he explains. "During the Battle of Armageddon, many buildings crumbled from earthquakes and volcanic explosions. Fires destroyed crops and forests." He sighs with reflection. "Like Earth was heaving and angrily lashing out."

"I'm lucky I wasn't living then."

Our family represents the fourth generation of the man known as Cory Lindsey. A simple soul who embraced Christianity and lived his life according to the Ten Commandments. His wife, Mary Jewel Sellers, is iconic in the world of Christian history. She was said to have walked past the sick and healed them by her very presence—something demonstrated by Peter, one of the Twelve Apostles who first followed Jesus Christ and His teachings. As was Peter's acts of faith, Mary's demonstrations of mercy were empowered by the Holy Spirit.

Thus, I have a legacy of faith-walkers in *The Way*.

My father taught me from infancy about the importance of reading the Holy Bible and obeying New Testament principles taught by Jesus Christ. I've studied our family history, a legacy in which my father takes pride. Our family has followed The Way since the return of Christ, and have always been students of the Ten Commandments.

How my father watches me makes me wonder what he is thinking. I've been told, a man is an island unto himself. I have bright eyes like my father—a violent-blue. His shimmers like crystals in the candlelight. Our visions are a genetic gift from my great grandmother, Mary Sellers, first married to Lucas Ralston who was taken in the Rapture when millions of people were snatched from the earth. Thought to be beamed up by space aliens, people learned differently after seven years of tribulation, a time of horror and death on earth.

It's all written down in our family journals, history now.

"Father, I want to travel to Jerusalem to see how it looks."

When Jesus' feet touched down on the Mount of Olives, the land split from east to west. Valleys were formed to the north and south as the city was raised to great heights. At the same time, a great upheaval every place else on earth took place, crumbling modern buildings, crashing communications, and destroying all modern conveniences.

There were few electric grids or windmills, no gas pipelines, to power homes. No cellphones or satellites to transmit information. The earth became nearly desolate. Many died. Few that survived suffered.

Over the first century, After Christ's Return, or ACR, trees and vegetation in desolate places began growing back. Time was reset to clock off the one-thousand-year kingly reign of Christ.

"That's a noble idea, son, seeking to view Jerusalem and visiting the Temple. You need to seriously pray about making this trip."

"I will, Father." I'd heard Jerusalem shines so brightly at night that darkness is diminished. Oh, it must have been a glorious day for Christians on earth when the Tribulation and Old Testament Saints returned wrapped in God's glory. My mind is so full of information, I am having trouble focusing now that I'm sure I am going to Jerusalem.

My father is speaking to me so I must concentrate.

"Traveling alone will be a dangerous, son," Joseph says. "The land itself is your enemy. I would go with you—except for this problem."

He points to his right leg. It was amputated three years ago due to a nasty infection from a rusty nail he accidentally stumbled upon.

"I'm not afraid, Father—to make the trip when I am ready."

"And not until you reach the age of sixteen. You must be mature and healthy to endure the journey. You will cross rivers, mountains, and a large body of water before you reach your destiny. Not everyone has embraced Christ's teachings. Some people will oppose you."

"I know it won't be easy, father." My mind skips to another thought. "My good friend Milo told me that his father made the journey across the ocean in a large boat built by the Egyptians."

"Hearsay, son. I know that family. The man did not return. No one knows what happened to him, or if he actually visited the city."

"I will succeed, Father. I know it for certain. God has called me in the night to come there and see His Magnificent Son Jesus."

Joseph musses David's mass of unruly red curls, a stark contrast to his blue eyes. His son's cheeks are dotted with freckles, reminiscent of the photographs Joseph has seen of Cory Lindsey. David is far from perfect, but like King David, he has a heart for God.

"I am so proud of you, son. You know the Bible backwards and forwards and comprehend what has been foretold by Old Testament prophets like Isaiah, Jeremiah, and Daniel. Your prayer life excels mine. I, too, know that you have the strong will to succeed."

"You must teach me all the skills I need to survive this journey. I am not like those who live in the City of Lights. I can't appear and disappear like the angels, or live forever like the Saints. I am just a boy, sometimes sick or injured," I tell him. "But I have faith in God."

"Yet, knowing your limitations, you still want to go."

"Yes. My faith overcomes all fear. I will never be the man God wants be to be if I don't do this and seek to worship the Lord."

I cannot help but smile.

"What is it, son?" Joseph rests his hand on my shoulder.

"The Apostle Paul said it so much better in Scripture than I can." I laugh hard. "My faith is like the substance of things hoped for, the evidence that cannot be seen." I pause. "You know what I mean."

"Yes, son, I know exactly." Joseph fears his only offspring has no inkling what he will endure venturing into the wilderness. From his understanding of Old Testament prophecy, only the elect will be able to travel the Highway of Holiness stretching from Egypt to Israel.

"I know you are afraid for me to travel alone, Father, but the Holy Spirit will guide me. How can Satan or his demons stop me when they are locked up? Besides, I have you to pray for me."

"Satan has his followers!" Joseph spouts. "People still walk upon this earth that reject the authority of Christ. They have chosen not to obey the Ten Commandments and live their lives sinfully."

Joseph knew of one village on the Atlantic coast that practiced idolatry. During their worship, they offered human sacrifices to their false god. Near the end, Satan will be loosed and lead a rebellion against Christ's reign. All life on earth will end. Then the judgment.

"I'm not afraid of anything, Father."

"I know you're not, but I promised your mother on her dying bed that I would guard your life. You are the only survivor in our family. You must find a suitable bride, marry, and produce offspring."

"Perhaps after I return from my trip."

Joseph sighs. His young son is so enthusiastic—a bit shy and naïve in many ways. This trip will be an eye-opener to how society works.

"Okay, then I guess it's settled, Father."

Joseph nods. "When you are sixteen, you will travel to see the City of Lights. Be mindful, it might take a year to get there. You must first reach the coast and find passage to Europe. There are requirements to enter into God's Presence. You will travel the Way of Holiness, a highway that begins in Egypt. Angels will qualify you."

"To see if I am good enough to bow before Jesus?"

"More to examine your soul to see if it is pure. God allows no sin in His Presence. Jesus is holy. His mercy is unending."

The idea of holiness chills me to the bone. I must be even more vigilant and study the Scriptures daily, pray more, and seek God's guidance before I embark on such a dangerous journey.

"I see I have frightened you, David. But you need to know how serious a quest you are undertaking. I will prepare you for your journey the best that I can—teach you what skills I know like constructing a tent from natural elements, or foraging food and locating fresh water."

"Thank you, Father, that is all I ask," I tell him. "Mama can rest in her grave. I am solely resting in the Power of the Holy Spirit."

"I know, son . . ."

"But what, Father?"

"Never mind, we will cross any obstacles when the time comes."

Six more years until June 16th before I will turn sixteen. I can hardly wait to be a man, but growing up takes time. Too much time.

Joseph hugged David. "Go to bed now. We have work to do tomorrow. I have in mind cutting down some trees and chopping wood for our fires this winter." The weather patterns were changing.

# 172 ACR

## 2

**"WILL I EVER SEE** that city?" I had asked my father the day I turned ten. After Christ's Return, earth drastically changed. The City of Lights became the focus of the world. Promises God made to Moses and the Israelites were being fulfilled on earth. People living in the Promised Land were living into their hundreds, just like they did before God destroyed the First World by a great flood that covered the planet.

Israeli children play safely in the streets, no bombs going off like it did in a hostile world. War between countries is forbidden, and no leader of any nation wants to test the authority of Christ Jesus.

Yet, I know rebellion against Christ's Kingdom exists. But I don't want to dwell on the negative. I am joyful today. The sun is shining brightly on this June morning. Tomorrow, I am turning sixteen and will leave on my long journey for Jerusalem. Excitement mounts.

"You can only enter the city by invitation," I recall my father's words. That statement gives me pause as I pack for the trip, many memories impact my mind all at once. How much will I miss home?

*Which angel will qualify me to enter the Highway of Holiness?*

According to the tenets of my village nestled at the foothills of the basin of the Guiana Highlands in Brazil, I become a man at sixteen and am expected to marry and begin my own family unit. Except I am breaking protocol with my village leaders since I have chosen to leave the settlement. Many have condemned my travel plans as foolish.

"Ha, you think you're any different from the last person that dashed off to the City of Lights?" one of Father's friends asked me.

*Am I foolish for trying to please God?*

It's been forty years since anyone from my village made this difficult journey. Even if I succeed, I don't know what I'll face when I return. Will people look at me funny? Will they think I think I am better than they are? Because I saw Jesus?

Lingering in my thoughts is the mystery of what happened to the last person who started out for Jerusalem. Did the journey take him? Or does he live in the City of Lights, growing older and wiser each day?

A rippling chill courses my spine as I consider the dangers I'll face. There are villages along the way where dissenters live. Offspring of non-Christians who oppose the rule of Jesus Christ. They refuse to bow down to Christ, or accept His supreme authority over Earth.

I imagine where these dissenters live is a desolate place. No rain falls on their dry soil. How can they drink salty ocean water?

It's a place I want to avoid.

*If I'll let them alone, will they bother me?*

I wish that all these thoughts were not colliding at this moment. Will the Holy Spirit sense doubt in me? Yet, I am positive I've heard Jesus calling me in the night: *Come to me, my son.*

"Does Jesus know about me?" is another question I'd asked my father on my tenth birthday. "Will He speak to me personally?"

Joseph is a good father, upright and honest. He would never lie to anyone, so I expected an honest answer, and he gave me one.

"Our Lord knows everything. He created you for a purpose at this time, David. The Prophet Isaiah said it best on behalf of God: *Remember what happened long ago, for I am God, and there is no other. I am God and no one is like Me. I declare the end from the beginning, and from long ago what is not yet done, saying, My plan will take place, and I will do all my will.*"

"Where is that scripture found in the Bible?" I had inquired.

"Isaiah 46: 9-10. Memorize those words, son. They will comfort you when life happens in ways you do not expect. Do not be foolish like so-called brilliant men who walked this earth before the Second Coming. People have no control over earth—not the rain, the snow, the frost, or heat. Humankind quickly learned their puny efforts to control the climate failed. *Yahweh* is the Author of the universe and has created all things for His pleasure. Jesus has authority over the earth."

This memory comforts me in ways I don't understand. As I prepare to make the journey to worship Jesus, I trust that God knows my every desire, my intent to humbly bow before Christ. Trust is important. Confession of sin, necessary. Good works, required.

And above all, mercy represents the essence of Christ.

When I was much younger, I tried to imagine the size of earth. All I knew about the cities that existed before Christ's return were from the pictures Father showed me in printed books. Hard copies that had been handed down through generations by our family.

After the War of Armageddon, the battle fought between Jesus and Satan, a great upheaval in the land had occurred. North and South poles were reset at different angles, changing how the sun heats the planet. My ancestors in Tennessee recognized that North America was becoming a cold wasteland, and that living in South America was their best chance of survival. Many people from America migrated south.

It's been reported that the northern half of the United States is iced over much of the year. Few plants grow anywhere north of Atlanta, Georgia. This makes me wonder about the weather in Israel.

*Is there a supernatural heating system?*

Great-grandfather Cory Lindsey four generations ago was among the first Tennesseans to make the journey South of the Border into Mexico with his family. They kept on going and settled in an isolated location where streams of clear water flowed from the mountains.

There, Cory's family found animals to hunt, vegetation for food and medicine, and a warmer climate. This settlement was close to Angel Falls, a waterfall so high one cannot see the top from its base.

Bethel is also our home. A burial site called, "The Estate of Souls" is where we bury our dead. As a youngster, the cemetery name seemed odd, but after my father educated me on the history of our clan, I understood the significance of the name. Souls are all that remain after physical death. Flesh decays. But one day all dead will rise to face God's judgment. Death is a transition from one type of life to another.

*From glory to glory, for even the angels study humanity.*

A Bema Banquet has already occurred in the City of Lights. I can only imagine what that was like. Saved people, transformed physically during the Rapture, gathered with all of the Angelic Host to celebrate the return of Christ to earth. At that time, Jesus rewarded Christians for their good deeds on earth. On the contrary, evil sinful people whose souls are not redeemed by the blood of Christ through God's merciful grace are kept in a place called Hades to await final judgment.

John the Revelator made it clear that earth will be destroyed by a massive fire at the end of the Millennium. God will create new skies, stars, and planets. A different form of life will exist on the New Earth. It will be a heavenly place without guilt, suffering, or sadness. This I've learned from my father or read in our historic Family Journals.

Now, it is my turn to be a man and act on my faith.

No two people walk the same path in this world. All I can be sure of is that I will enter Jerusalem and bow before King Jesus and declare God's majesty. I cannot imagine how all that will play out.

After finishing packing my lunch, I started my two-hour journey to the village closest to mine, Jupiter. There is a girl living there I like very much. Well, *love*, to be honest. I want to say goodbye to her.

*Will she wait for me to return and marry me?*

It's a lot to ask of any woman. But if she agrees, we are looking at least two years of separation, maybe more. I will tell her that after three years, if I don't return to my village, she is free to marry another.

My heart pounds at what will happen when we meet. It's a wilderness walk to Jupiter, but I know the way since I've often been there since turning thirteen. Dahlia is dazzling. She has radiant auburn hair, a sprinkling of tan freckles on her plump rosy cheeks, and green eyes like rare stones. *Emeralds,* I recall. She is an enchanting creature.

Time passes quickly as I reach my destination and kneel behind a bush to watch her hang wet clothes on a cotton rope stretched between two limbs. I'm speechless at seeing her. Struck dumb, to be honest.

As if sensing my presence, she turns around and smiles. I step into full view, feeling a bit foolish for hiding. Am I blushing?

"David? I'm surprised to see you again so soon."

She walks toward me as my heart leaps.

"Did you send word you were coming today?"

"No, I—did you forget tomorrow is my birthday?"

We embrace as I lean forward to kiss her on the forehead. I am six feet two inches tall and weigh as much as a small deer. I am proficient at many skills, thanks to my father. I use a bow like a lethal weapon to kill meat for our village. We have a barter system since paper money is worthless—although some keep the green stuff.

"No, I did not forget, David. Your birth date is on my Calendar of Days. I was coming to see you tomorrow afternoon."

We stand there, just staring at one another. I am starstruck as Dahlia removes a small rag wrapped around something mysterious in her apron pocket. "You'll have to wait till tomorrow to get this."

"Tomorrow is too late," I say.

"Surely, you jest."

I love how she sassily parks a hand on one hip.

"I'm not. I won't be at home when you arrive." My lips are dying to touch hers. "I leave for my trip to the City of Lights at dawn."

"You've come to say goodbye." She wears her emotions on her face. A devastation of unhappiness at my departure.

"What about out your village's celebration of manhood."

"It will have to wait until I return. If I don't leave tomorrow, I will encounter a harsh winter as I venture north."

I grieve at seeing Dahlia's disappointment.

"Oh, David!" She throws herself against me, like I am about to evaporate. "I'll be so lonely while you are away. Take me with you. I'll be no trouble, I promise." There is much passion in her green gaze.

I put her at arm's length. I do not trust my desire to bed her to diminish. But I honor her virginity. Dahlia is only three inches shorter than me. A mammoth female in her generation. One of her male ancestors was a general in the American Army, I've been told. His wife said to have won many beauty contests in the State of Montana.

There are tears in Dahlia's eyes. I slowly dry them with a hand.

"Don't be sad, sweetheart." I open my right hand to reveal a glittering gold ring. "This was my grandmother's—God rest her soul."

She examines the ring then looks at me.

"Is this what I think it means, David?"

"Yes, it's a tribute to our friendship. Will you marry me?"

She laughs and spins around like a mythical fairy.

"You are not surprised." I grasp her hand to steady her. "You knew I would come today and ask you to marry me."

She punches me on the chest. "If you hadn't, young man, I would have asked you. But now you've beaten me to the punch."

Her eyes light up like candles.

"So, you'll marry me?"

"Yes, I'll marry you."

We kiss, longer than any time before. I am elated that Dahlia is mine. She belongs to no other man. We will create our own family.

"There can be no ceremony until I return." I set down a rule.

"We could marry before you leave."

"No, I don't want to leave you after our ceremony."

"I thought you'd say that." Dahlia's smile faded. "All you've talked about for three years is this trip." She sighs. "And I accept those terms. Reluctantly. But I will gladly wait for your return."

"It's a lot to ask of any woman."

"I know, but love binds."

# 3

**TODAY IS JUNE 16ᵀᴴ.** I am packed and ready to leave for "The City of Lights." If Jerusalem is known by any other name, I will find out when I get there. I have much to learn on my long journey halfway across the world. I've seen Father's metallic globe, so know that traveling on foot will take time.  If I am fortunate, I will hitch a ride on a wagon. Or a boat—like the Spanish-born Columbus who sailed across the Atlantic Ocean and discovered the Americas. Like the famous explorer, few from our parts of the country have gone before me.

According to the sundial located in the middle of our village, the sun will move into view over the mountain in approximately thirty minutes, give or take. I've been told that in modern days of old, citizens of the world read the time on their phones. I cannot imagine using a tool like that.  In magazines so old they feel like crisp venison. I have seen pictures of these iPhones. These tools worked because great moon-like balls circled the globe to connect them. A huge asteroid struck the moon and cluttered our atmosphere. Most of these so-called satellites fell to the ground. People in those days used these phones to stay in contact. Nothing like that works in our world today.

All that is left of modern technology is hearsay.

While I am checking my gear and determining how much I can carry on my back, all these thoughts flood my mind.  In some way, I want to marry Dahlia and live an ordinary life in our village.  But I cannot ignore the call of Christ to come and see Him in Jerusalem.

I am on my knees praying to God for safety in the coming days, weeks, and months as the sun slips over the mountain and melts the darkness.  I come to my feet, strap my gear on my back, and cast one last look at my father's house.  Merely a lean-to with a grassy roof.

My eyes blink with tears as I follow a trail leading upward from our village and through a mountain pass.  I have a compass to guide me in my journey.  Enough food for three days, then I will need to hunt. Since Christ's return, animals seem to be at peace with humans.

*Am I afraid a lion might change his mind and eat me?*

Casting away foolishness, I begin singing: *Here am I, Lord.  Send me.* This song reminds me of the Prophets of Old, always willing to go where the LORD leads them.  I want to be brave like them.

* * *

The first day ended in a torrential rainstorm.  I took cover in a cave on the other side of the mountain from my village, estimating I had walked a good thirty miles.  For some less athletic males, this pace would be impossible.  But I have trained for this trip since childhood.

*I have weight-lifted logs the size of small elephants.*

I suddenly laugh at my description as I imagine that scene.

It is hot and humid tonight. Rain pours down the sides of the cave and rustles off below me. The fire I lit warms my heart more than my sweaty body. The jungle beneath speaks volumes from a variety of disturbed animals scurrying to find dry spaces in the ground, high in trees, or in caves carved into the multi-sides of the mountain.

My eyes are heavy with sleep as I read the New Testament my father presented me yesterday for my sixteenth birthday.  I recall the sadness resting in his gaze.  There is great love there for me.  And concern for my safety.  But I trust God to see me safely to the City of Lights.  At that thought, I lay my head against the rock and sleep.

* * *

I am awakened the second morning by a squirrel scampering up my pants.  "Whoa!" I startle as the little creature chatters.  It has a fist-full of nuts in his mouth and stares at me like I am a friend.

"Are these for me?" I reach out and grab two.

The creature chatters and races away.

I laugh hard, reminded of how God rained down manna from Heaven to feed the Israelites in the Sinai Desert on their journey to the Promised Land.  I crack the nut with my teeth and devour the inside.

The nut tastes sweet and meaty.  "Thank you, squirrel," I utter.

On my feet again, with my heavy backpack attached, I collect fresh water flowing down from the mountain.  I am thirsty, so I drink heartily.  The morning feels cooler, with less humidity.  The rainstorm has passed, so I anticipate a beautiful day for travel.  With my goal in mind, I climb down and follow a trail of someone who has gone before me, wondering where it will lead.  Then I take off running.

* * *

At noon, I come upon a rushing river I presume is headed for another tributary that will eventually empty into the Atlantic Ocean.

I glance around for material to create a raft.  I will need logs and strong blades of sugarcane to tie them together. So, I get busy.

By mid-afternoon, I am floating down the river, taking in the changing terrain as I leave the mountainous forest for flat plains.

I'm not in control of where I float, but I am not worried.  Progress is all that matters. Keep moving toward the great water. There will be villages there. And people who can help me. Or kill me.

# 4

## Four Days Later

**I AM ON FOOT** again, walking toward the largest village I have ever seen. There must be a thousand huts clustered alongside a body of water with such expanse I cannot see the other side. Behind me the sun is setting, casting long shadows over the thatched roofs. I feel excitement, thinking this body of water must be the Atlantic Ocean.

I offer a prayer up to God that the residents of this community of survivors are friendly. I need to replenish my supplies, including food, and find safe passage to Europe across the deep troubled waters.

There's a path leading down to the village. I follow it, so tired I am about to drop. I estimate I've traveled for more than four-hundred kilometers counting the time spent on my river raft.

The day has closed down and turned to night. I feel safer under the cloak of darkness as I walk. Very few people are still out on the network of passages leading between rows of huts. Through small openings in the sides of the huts I see light, probably from candles. This village, though many times larger than mine, has similar traits.

I hear the laughter of children as I make my way toward the ocean. I want to see if there are boats docked there. My father showed me pictures in magazines of great seafaring vessels. Do they still exist?

Two tall men walk toward me. They are busy conversing, so with my head down they barely note my passing. Good, I fit in somehow.

I have no idea what time it is, but I guestimate somewhere around nine o'clock. It's mid-summer in South America, so daylight lasts longer than darkness. I need to find a place to rest till morning.

Thinking my feet can no longer carry me a step farther, I spy an opening at the end of rows of thatched huts. There is a long dock with boats sinking and rising in motion on top of the frothing water.

I like the smell of the ocean, the scent of fish—which makes me hungry. "Ho! Who comes?" I hear a deep voice call out. Then see a large bulky man step into view as he stands on the surface of a boat.

I wave at him. "Ho! May I come aboard?"

He waves me toward him. "Yah, I know you not."

He speaks funny—likes he's a foreigner from some distant shore.

"Kin I he'p you, young man?"

"Yes, thank you kindly." I approach him and stand at the base of the boat. It's much larger than it appeared at a distance.

"So . . .?" His head bobbles and his thick beard shimmers from the burning candle he holds in his left hand. "State yo'r bus'ness."

"I am from a village at the base of the Guiana Highlands, near Angel Falls. Have you heard of it?" I wait for his response.

"Yah, tis a far distance from here."

"You talk funny."

He laughs. "As do ye."

"Where are you from?"

"Israel."

I suddenly feel the Holy Spirit rush through me, leaving me tingling all over. "Ah, do you plan to go home anytime soon?"

"Yah, soon as my boat can sail."

"You are Jewish."

"Yah."

"Do you need help repairing your boat? I'm good at carpentry."

"Ya' look healthy, son. Hav' ya sailed before?"

"No, but what I don't know, you can teach me."

He bobbles his large head. Eyes are black holes in his rugged face, hovering under his bushy-gray eyebrows. I imagine he looks like one of the Old Testament prophets I've read about in the Bible.

"I am a Christian. I want to go to Jerusalem to see the King."

"Yah, tis a long way to travel. Many dan'gers. You sure?"

"I've heard Jesus calling me in the night to worship Him."

The old sailor smiles for the first time—if you can call the crack in his parched lips stretched between two plump cheeks that. His crooked front teeth are tobacco-stained and partially rotted. But I like him. And I believe we can work something out if I'm clever.

"So . . . this is why I've been sent," he utters, removing a pipe from his shirt as he sets the stout candle on the rocking boat deck.

"What do you mean?" I am bowled over by his remark.

"Three yeers—maybe fo'r—I woke up en the night and I heard a voice say, 'Benjamin, take a trip to the Americas.'" He grins.

I blink with understanding. "You were sent here."

"Yah, by the King."

"For me?"

"For ya—it seems so now." He heartily laughs.

"I don't know what to say."

"Come aboard, son, we have much to talk about."

I nod, then grab onto his calloused hand and board the boat.

"How can I thank you, Benjamin?"

"Ye thank me by com'in. I'm weary of wait'in."

I laugh hard. God always makes a way.

# 5

**MORNING DAWNED WITH** glorious color as the sun melted its glow over the troubled waters of the breathing ocean. I'd always believed that the mountains were God's most beautiful creation, but I see now that a sunrise runs a close first. I think for a moment where I am.

I rise from my straw bed in the porthole to my feet, yawn, and glance around me. The odors of decaying wood and fish overwhelm me. A few minutes later, I join Benjamin topside on the ship deck.

"Did'ja hav' a good sleep, son?"

"The best," I reply, inhaling a delicious cooking odor.

"Hop' ya like fish fer breakfast."

He sits on an oil can, grilling his catch of the morning over some black coals glowing under a flat black skillet. His grin refreshes me.

"I could eat a possum, sir. Bring it on!" I laugh.

The Jew reminds me of a grizzly bear, but his personality is more like a gentle lamb. He's someone I might identify with Santa Claus—if I believed in fairytales. He's someone my father would like.

"Sit a spell, son, and eat. We hav' work to do."

As I fold my legs and settle on the deck, a cool breeze gently rocks the boat. My breakfast comes on a flat wooden, hand-carved dish.

"Shall we thank Yahweh?'

I bow my head as Benjamin says a prayer in Hebrew. I wish I'd paid more attention to my father's advice that I study languages to greater extent. I'm out in the world now and understanding what is said around me could save my life. The long prayer ends.

"That was nice," I comment.

"Ya' did no' understand a word I said." He laughs.

"No, but I'm sure that Yahweh did."

We both laugh.

"Well, eat yo'r food, son. No more till dark."

Hands are our utensils. His are grubby with oil and wood stains while mine are more refined. I feel somewhat guilty for my prosperity.

"The fish is great! What kind of seasoning?" I inquire.

"It's an ol' recipe handed down in my fam'ly."

"I'm always interested in family heritage, what's yours?"

"My, my, lad. Ye pro'bly don' hav' the time for a hist'ry lesson." Benjamin laughs, water sloshing from his tin cup.

"No, I really want to hear about your life." I stand to my feet and toss my fishbones into the foaming salty water below us.

"Ah then, wha' kin I tell ya?"

"Has Israel always been your family home?"

"Nay, son. my great-great grandfather was born in Palestine. Many say only Muslims live in that part of the country. Not so."

"It seems that way, based on what I've read about the conflict between Israel and Palestine." I roll my shoulders, my muscles tight and needing exercise. I am used to hard labor and my trip was long.

"Ya' ve read the Bible, son. Ya' know Jesus often visited Palestine. Paul the Apostle evangelized many Jews from that part of Israel to accept Jesus as their savior. Back then, my ancestors were Jewish priests, descendants of the Prophet Amos. Some rejected the Word."

"Really?" His story keeps getting better.

"Ya', wher' do ya' think I get my prophetic gifts?"

I smile, no words to express my awe at Benjamin's heritage. I can learn much from this man about the Nation of Israelites.

"Le's take a walk into the city." Benjamin rises to his feet, dousing the hot coals with the rest of the liquid in his cup.

"What's there?" I puzzle.

"Supplies to purchase fer our ocean cruise." He chuckles at his statement. "I heer people us'ta pay for a chance to sail the high seas."

"A cruise," I recall and laugh hard. "I saw some of those gigantic sailing vessels pictured in an old magazine my father kept."

"Eh? Ya, 'tis funny now, but folks back then took recreation seriously. They paid big bucks for their sailing experience."

"I wonder what happened to all those ocean liners."

"Tribulation trials eventually took ever'thing down."

"Satellites eyes in the sky, and modern technology that powered those ships." I suddenly feel the urge to pee. "You have a privy?"

"Nay, 'tis one in the square. Bes' we be goin' now."

It was a fifteen-minute walk from the wharf to the epicenter of Jamestown. Some history buff from America had decided the name suited the new settlement some century-and-a-half ago when he first arrived to the coast. The open market area was bustling with people, wares for sale like homemade products such as clothing and useful things for the home. Few artifacts were for sale; mostly necessities.

I found the public privy and relieved myself. Outdoors, I spied Benjamin across the street in front of the blacksmith's shop having a conversation with a tall, skinny black man. I'd seen few negroes in Brazil, but I knew the black race inhabited much of the African Continent. Benjamin was involved in a heated conversation.

I wandered over, not wanting to get directly involved. But if the need came to defend Benjamin, I was up to the task.

He came away from the blacksmith frowning.

"What was that all about?" I inquire.

"He doesn't have th' material to make the part I need fer my boat engine," Benjamin explains as we turn back toward the coastline.

"We can't sail without it?"

"Nay, son. Closest village is not a good place."

"What do you mean?"

"Not safe, son. Real bad folks live ther'."

"What makes them bad?"

"Witchcraft. Folks in Rebellion practice witchcraft."

"I thought Jesus made it clear sorcery is forbidden."

"Our Savior did, son. But they rebelled."

I nod, finally understanding the name given to the settlement.

"Why are you telling me this, Benjamin?"

"We need a boat part made there by a blacksmith known as Black Beard—like the thief that sailed the High Seas back when."

"I never heard of the man. Was he famous?"

"Ya, in a bad sort of way. I'm sorry but it 'peers I need ya to go ther' and buy the part," he says. "Is it too much to ask?"

"I don't think I have a choice if we sail the High Seas."

# 6

**I SET OUT FOR** Rebellion late morning. It's a four-hour walk, about fifteen kilometers if you hustle your steps. The sandy soil is hot and flat along the coastline, but easier to walk than up and down mountainous terrain. I'll need to find shelter for the night when I get there since it will be dark before I can complete my task. I'll need to find the blacksmith and make my request for Benjamin's boat part.

And I have no idea what to expect when I get there.

Before I left Jamestown, Benjamin asked about my family heritage. I shared with him as much as I could recall in the moment. Any prophetic gifts I have stem back to Mary Lindsey, hailed by Christians for her acts of evangelism and healing before Christ's return.

Samantha Golden, my grandmother, was in her lineage.

The sun burns down hotter as I get closer to Rebellion. Benjamin warned me that it hasn't rained on the village in more than fifty years, since the last person left for Jerusalem to offer worship to the King.

I recall a passage of scripture in 1 Kings where the Prophet Elijah faced off with King Ahab's chief minister regarding Jezebel's slaughtering of 100 Israeli priests. Obadiah reported to Ahab that Elijah wanted a meeting. Ahab found Elijah and confronted him.

"Destroyer to Israel!" Elijah accused Ahab because he'd destroyed Israel by abandoning the Lord's commandments and followed after the Baals. "Let's see whose god is greater," Elijah had challenged him.

King Ahab summoned the Israelites and Baal prophets to meet at Mount Carmel. Elijah asked how long the people would serve Baal. He was the only prophet left that had not been killed by Queen Jezebel.

Believing in God's power to outmatch witchcraft, Elijah challenged the 400 Baal prophets to make it rain. They couldn't.

I know from my reading that the Baal religion revolves around the cycles of nature necessary for survival and the prosperity in the ancient world—primarily growing crops or raising livestock, as well as growth of human populations. The religion evolved from a myth about a god called Marduk who brought order to the universe after it had been split in two. Marduk represents order in the forces of nature, like spring with its renewal of life and energy to Earth. The Baal religion is based on this myth. He is the "Rider of the Clouds," an imagery associated with rain and storms. One of the worship rituals involves sex with temple prostitutes, an act to procreate life. The people of Rebellion worship the false god Baal since rain has not fallen in five decades.

Elijah won the contest against the 400 false prophets of Baal when he summoned rain to fall on Samaria. God rained down fire to destroy the altar prepared by the false prophets. God made His point.

*I am Yahweh and no god is greater than I AM.*

My feet burn through the soles of my sandals as I grow closer to my destination. My lips are parched and I'm powerfully thirsty. The last water from my canteen is gone and my stomach growls for food.

As I approach the village, I note there is a tall, gated entrance. A very large man stands guard. I have no option but to approach him.

"State your business," he says.

His voice rumbles like deep waters. I'm not usually afraid of anything or anyone, but this hairy guy is creepy. I consider my answer.

"Your tongue has been cut out?" He barks.

Startled by his comment, I say, "No, I'm here to see the blacksmith about a boat part. Where can I find him?"

"Turn around and go back from where you came."

I didn't move but his message is clear. *Get lost!*

"I can't do that," I tell him. "You have a name?"

"Thor."

"That makes sense."

He scratches his bald head and it makes me think of Goliath the Giant—not that I'm any David with a slingshot. Thor must be eight-feet tall and weighs close to five-hundred pounds—no match for me.

I feel a tug at my pants leg and look down. The smallest man I've ever seen stands there. He's fully grown, but no taller than a toddler.

"You need to find Blackbeard."

His voice is odd, but stronger than I'd expect.

I nod. "Will you show me the way?"

"NO!" Thor bellows.

The midget looks up at the giant with oversized bug eyes in his big head, not proportioned to the size of his small, muscular body.

"He's with me, Thor.  Get out of my way or I'll tell your wife about the temple prostitute you sleep with every Sunday."

The giant grits his teeth but he moves out of our way.  I consider the midget a gift from God to get me inside the village.

"You have a name?" I ask the little man as we pass through the gate and enter a village that looks a lot like Jamestown.  But I am reminded of Benjamin's warning: *Bad folks live there.*

"Stump," the midget replies.  "Because I didn't grow."

I smile at the little guy. "That makes perfect sense."

Stump takes me to the wharf where fishermen are hauling in their catches of the day.  He slips under a wire that cordons off a section of the beach.  "Wait here and I'll get our supper," he instructs me.

I'm not about to contest any method of obtaining food, short of stealing since I won't break one of God's Ten Commandments.  I sit down in the sand and wait for my supper to be served by a new friend.

Rebellion faces the east, so the sun is setting behind me.  A crimson color washes over the ocean water and streams outward.  I thank God I've come this far to Israel—though it's still a long way off.

Stump returns with two paper-wrapped grilled cod and dumps one in my lap.  "Eat then we'll find shelter."  He sits across from me.

"Do you have a home?"

"Every shadow is my home, David."

"How do you know my name, Stump?"

"Word gets around. Believe it or not, I am a Christian."

I blink with understanding.

"I know—a saint among sinners."  He chuckles.

"I was told this village has bad people."

His plump cheeks are filled with food as he mutters an answer, "Not all are bad.  My parents were Christians. Dead now."

"What happened to them?" I taste my fish for the first time. "Delicious.  Do I need to pay you for the food?"

"If you have gold, keep it hidden," Stump warns. "Folks provide me with food because I'm an outcast.  Outcast is sometimes good.  Nobody pays attention to me when I don't participate in Baal rituals."

"You speak English well, Stump.  Are you educated?"

"Yes, my parents were Christian missionaries."

"How did they die?" I finish my supper and discard the bones.

"Sacrificed to Baal." He brushes salt from his small hands. "Eat, friend, and let's find shelter before night falls. No moon out tonight."

"Okay, but I have a lot of questions about your culture."

"Let's get moving. The giants come after dark to sleep here."

"Like Thor." I nod.

"He has a home. Others. Ancestors from Norway. They brag about the wars their clan waged. But they don't mess with me."

"Because you know their secrets." I nod.

He chuckles. "My only weapon against the giants."

# 7

**I WAKE UP IN** a pop-up tent, the canvas over me almost touching my nose.  Stump is still sleeping, snoring gourds.  I crawl out of the tent and realize the sounds of the village are already stirring.

*What is today?*  Thursday, I believe.

I'm thirsty and hungry again. One thing is certain about the human body: it always craves nourishment.  My thoughts are banging around in my head like a boomerang.  I need to find the blacksmith.

Stump crawls out of the tent. "Morning."

"Yes, it is—by the way, why did you decide to help me?"

"No choice."  He hops around and shakes his body.

"That doesn' make any sense," I pose.

"Came in a dream.  David Goldman is coming. Help him."

"An angel spoke to you?"

"No, your name was a voice in my dream."

I didn't want to irritate the little guy, so I accepted his explanation.

"How can I find the blacksmith?" I ask.

"Follow me."

His short legs move like a rodent scurrying across a pathway.  Finally, I snag him by his shirt and set him on one shoulder.

"Now, just tell me where to go," I declare.

"Walk to the end of this street and take a right," Stump points.

I feel the stares of people as we walk.  They recognize a stranger because few get past Thor.  And they wonder why I am here.

"Go left." Stump points.  "At the end of this street."

I obey, hoping what I find at the end of our journey is not a knife in my heart.  Surely, Jesus will protect us both since He has planned so well for my coming.  I need to rest in my faith that I'm safe.

We arrive at a large structure that looks like a cattle barn.  Two front wooden doors are laid back and I hear hammering inside.

"Put me down!" Stump orders, and I do.  "In there!"

"You're not coming with me?"

"I'm not crazy.  Should I die today with you?"

Stump scurries off and disappears in the crowd of people gathering in the street. I turn around and face another giant.

"WHO ARE YOU?"

Blackbeard's voice booms even louder than Thor's. He has a bushy black beard covering his chin. A scary—I won't say the word.

"David. I come from Jamestown to buy a boat part."

"How did you get past my brother?"

"Thor?"

He nods, a snarl tearing at his lips. He's bald like his brother and has a series of gold rings in his left ear. His naked upper Godzilla torso has been shaved and the hair replaced with a coiling snake tattoo.

"Stump brought me here," I barely utter.

His bulbous lips twist to one side in thought.

"Stump, you say. What do you need?"

I show Blackbeard the drawing Benjamin gave me. "It's something my friend needs to sail his boat."

He studies the drawing.

"Can you make the part?" I ask.

"Yeah, but it requires a special type rare metal."

"I have money to pay you," I hurriedly say.

He spits in the dust. "Don't take cash."

I smile.

"You think that's funny?"

"No, no . . ." I recall cash was useless during the Tribulation since the Mark was the only allowable currency. A chip was inserted in the wrist, the "Mark of Satan" Christians called it, since God's enemy ruled the world during that era. I retrieve a handful of gold coins from a small knapsack. "Will these do?" I show him my currency.

His grin is barely detectable.

"Okay, you come back tomorrow."

"Thank you." A load lifts off my back since I'm not dead.

"No, thank the gold!" He heartily laughs.

Turning around, realizing I'm footloose and free to wander the streets. *But is it safe?* I start back the way I came and end up at the wharf.

It's a busy day for fishermen. I don't see Stump anywhere.

"You should hide."

*Huh?* I turn around and face a young woman. *Beautiful!*

She has almond-shaped eyes, black as onyx. Silky lips like rubies, and curly blond hair tumbling to her waistline. She wears a white toga with sandals. Desirable comes to mind. I finally find my voice.

"Who are you?"

"Diana." She smiles. "I'm a temple prostitute."

The phlegm in my throat chokes me. She seems friendly, and obviously has singled me out. I don't know what to say to her. Should I tell her about Jesus? She's a sinner; yet she is here warning me.

"Cat got your tongue?"

She's toying with me. "Why should I hide?" A logical question.

"If the elders of Rebellion find you, they'll put you in jail and sacrifice you to Baal on Sunday." She's direct and the idea scares me.

"I don't know anyone here. Where can I hide?"

"You know me." Diana crooks a slender finger.

I have no other option but to follow her. Am I about to enter a trap? Will Diana try to seduce me? Can I trust her?"

I offer up a prayer to God for guidance.

"Your choice. Trust me or die," Diana states.

I nod then trail her away from the wharf and down a dark alley. We enter an old abandoned building—one that survived the upheaval of land during the Battle of Armageddon that followed Jesus' return.

"You live here?"

"No, but it's a good place for you to hide. The building has been condemned and villagers are banned from coming inside."

"It doesn't look unlivable—with a little fixing up—"

"Not possible!" Diana exclaims. "Christian missionaries ran an orphanage in this building. Baal worshippers consider the building unholy." She actually grins. "I know—sounds stupid, doesn't it?"

I stare into her mysterious eyes, wide and engaging. So black the universe might be hidden in them. Diana is desirable and I suddenly want to hug her. But the Holy Spirit cautions me to be careful.

"You want to lie with me." Diana clutches my arm.

Fire shoots through my body. This village is evil. Filled with devil worshippers and demon spirits. I want to run, but I cannot. I am drawn to Diana like a moth to fire. *God, help me resist her charm.*

I gently remove her arm. "I can't, Diana—not that I don't want to, but I am betrothed to another. But I thank you for your help."

Tears clouds her vision. "I only offered because I want to escape Rebellion. I was forced into prostitution. My parents were good, honorable people before they were sacrificed to Baal. Their blood ran in the streets and the dogs licked it up. I was spared—"

"Because of your beauty," I finished her statement.

She nods and I feel compassion toward her.

"Will you take me with you when you leave?"

"I don't know if I can, but I'll try," I say. "But no more solicitation from you. Okay?" She is a creature of marvelous beauty. Her skin is a creamy white, unblemished. Her figure is perfect.

"I don't even know your name," she says.

"David. David Goldman."

"Where are you from?"

"Jamestown," I reply, not wanting to reveal the location of my home, lest some of the Baal worshipers decide to seek revenge.

She nods. "Stay here. I will bring food and water."

I open my small cloth knapsack and hand her two gold coins.

She shakes her head. "Too much; one will do."

"No." I close the coins in her hand. "You keep one for yourself. Buy something that pleases you. You deserve more than this village has given you. I am so sorry you have been sexually abused."

I hear Diana's sniffles as she exits the building.

With nothing more to do than wait, I lean against a half-fallen wall and drift off to sleep. My dreams are sweet. I am holding Dahlia in my arms and I feel safe again. *Who can stand against me if the LORD is for me?* I recall a biblical scripture in the New Testament. Time passes.

I startle as a rough hand touches me. Then open my eyes. Stump stands there with a jug in one hand and a sandwich in the other.

"Diana told me you were here." He hands me my breakfast.

"Thank you." I chug down the water then unwrap my sandwich. Ham on rye bread with goat cheese. I take a huge bite, nearly choking as I blurt out, "Why did you desert me to deal with Blackbeard alone?"

"I can't babysit you all day, I have to work to do."

"What kind of work does a little guy like you do?" I devour the sandwich like it's my last meal and chug down some water.

"A lot of talking—the way I learn people's secrets," Stump replies.

"Bargaining for favors, I get it."

The midget grins. "Did you sleep with her?"

"Diana? No!" A scowl tears through my face.

"But she offered, right?"

I sigh. "She offered. Hard to turn down, I admit."

"She wants you to take her with you when you leave."

"How do you know that, Stump?" I wad the wrapping to my sandwich and toss it to the dirty stripped wooden floor.

A rat scurries between me and Stump. He curses.

"How do you know that, Stump?" I grab him by the shirt.

"She always does. One visitor tried to take her."

"Tried, but did not succeed?"

"No one steals a temple prostitute. It's a sin against Baal. The last guy that tried was burned to a stake. Don't do it."

I think about Stump's warning. I feel sorry for Diana. I want to help her, but even more, I need the part for Benjamin's boat.

*How else can I get to Jerusalem?*

# 8

# Friday

**I'D SPENT THE NIGHT** in the abandoned "forbidden-to-enter" building and, to my surprise, no one came to arrest or kill me. Today, I would return to Blackbeard's shop to see if he's made the device Benjamin needs for his boat. It is hot and dry when I hit the street.

Neither Diana or Stump are there to check on me—so much for tender-loving care in the city of sin. I began my trek toward the blacksmith's establishment, quoting Bible scriptures on my journey.

If looks could kill, I'm already dead. I envision being tied to a stake with a pile of dry wood under my feet and Thor flipping a torch to fry me. I wonder if the Baal worshippers eat their prey. Or if one of their priests might slice my neck and let me bleed out.

None if those scenarios calm my rapidly-beating heart. Seeing how the rebellious citizens of the village are steeped in drunkenness and adulterous sin makes me wonder how King Jesus puts up with humankind. Disputes and fights break out at any moment as I walk past men gathering like a flock of cocks to cluck and scratch.

There is little peace her. With negativism rippling like stones in my brain, I realize I am there. "YOU!"

I hear his words before my brain processes. "Thor!"

He's angry. Join the crowd. It's rubbing off on me.

His voice booms, "I thought I told you to leave!"

I swallow hard, pressed how best to respond.

"You did," I swallow, "but I need my boat part."

Why am I so stupid as to stand here communicating with a bully twice my size? A thug who obviously despises me for no other reason than I am a visitor to his fine village. "I'll leave soon, I promise."

He blinks with understanding then points over one shoulder

I lean to one side and peek past Thor's huge frame.

"Blackbeard told me you paid him," Thor says.

I nod. "Did he build my part?"

"I'm not your secretary!" Thor angrily remarks.

"No, of course not.  I'll just ask Blackbeard."

When Thor didn't move, I sigh.

"Is there something you want from me?" I inquire.

"Are you a Christian?" He studies me like I'm a bug he wants to squash with his size 20 sandals.

"I—uh . . ." Now, that's a million-dollar question whereby an honest answer could land me under a fire, in a boiling pot, or bleeding out at the neck. "Is that important, since I'm paying for my part?"

Moments feel like hours as I await my fate.

Thor snarls then tramps away in a cloud of dust. Relieved, I walk into the den of the blacksmith. The atmosphere turns dark and dismal with sickening odors, no sunlight through windows to light my way.

"Good morning!" I try to sound cheery.

But Blackbeard looks sick.

"I'm sorry, did you catch a cold?" I inquire.

"Worse!  I smell something holy in the air, and that always makes me sick."  He leans over and smells me.  "You stink."

*Thank God!* I rejoice over poor hygiene.

"I didn't get my shower this morning," I cleverly admit.

"I'll get your motor part."

So much easier than I anticipated.  I wait.

He returns and hands me a metal canister, a bit too heavy to carry during my walk back to Jamestown. "What's inside?" I ask.

"What you need."

"I don't even get a peek?"

"Don't open the box.  Trust me, if you do, it won't go well."

I meditate on Blackbeard's warning a nanosecond then decide it is in my best interest not to argue, rather walk away unharmed.

"I can go?"

"You can go."

I trek back through the village, eyes following me eagerly like I'm prime meat for their next dining experience. The metal box is heavy.

As I leave Rebellion, I spy a large building a quarter of a kilometer away on the beach.  A lot of activity is going on—none of my business.

I'm just happy to be out of touch with Baal worshippers.

Half way back to Jamestown, I limp to my right from carrying the metal box.  I need to rest.  That's when surprise slaps me in the face.

"Hi."

I glance back from the rock where I'm seated.

"You followed me?  Are you crazy!"

Diana the Temple Prostitute grins.

"Easy as eating pie."

I can tell she's enjoying needling me.

"Won't *they* come after you?" I utter.

"The Baal priests?  Sure, but I have you to protect me."

I stand up, hands raised defensively.  "I had nothing to do with you escaping.  You came out of Rebellion without my help."

She laughs.  "But *they* don't know that."

"Stump warned me not to trust you."

"Aw, are you trying to hurt my feelings, David?"  She folds her body under the shade of a tree.  "At least, it's rained here recently."

"Yeah, I noticed how dry it was around Rebellion."  I offer her a chunk of cheese I'd purchased on my way out of the village.

"Thanks, but I have my own food—have to watch my figure, you know."  She removes an apple from a knapsack and munches on it.

We are silent while we eat.

"What?"  I notice how she's staring at me.

"Shouldn't we be running?  They're coming."

Somehow, Diana's comment reminds me of a 1980's ghost movie the elders of my village played for our Saturday Show Night.  A little girl spied ghosts inside the static of her television.  *They're here . . .*

"You're right, we should not tarry."

She laughs.  "Finally, some respect."

"But . . . we should set some ground rules," I say.

"No touchy, no feely?"

"Not that. When we come to the fork in the road, you go right and I'll go left." I hook the rope to the heavy box over my left shoulder.

"What? You don't like my company?"

"It's not that," I say. "Hard to follow two people going different directions," I explain my decision.  But Diana isn't buying it.

"Wherever thou go'est, I will go."

I can't help from chuckling. "You actually quote a passage of scripture from the Book of Ruth?" My tongue nearly wags.

"I told you my folks were missionaries. I'm no savage."

"Okay, you've made your point, let's go."

We chose an alternate route through the wooded terrain instead of heading straight to the sandy beach. So, we didn't make it back to Jamestown before night caught up with us. We sheltered in a cave as it stormed outdoors. Diana stood at the opening with arms raised.

I wondered who she was praising. Maybe, she just liked the rain.

# 9

## Saturday

**I DIDN'T GET MUCH** sleep last night, but Diana snored with contentment. The rain had stopped and a cool breeze was stirring. I tapped her on the shoulder. "Wake up, Diana! We have to go now!"

She lazily rolls over and looks up at me. I want to swim in her lovely eyes—pools so dark and mysterious I knew why men loved her.

*Resist,* I warn myself. *You are engaged.*

"I'm hungry, what's for breakfast?"

"Get up, Diana, we'll find something to eat on our way."

"My, my, aren't you testy today." She stands up and raises her creamy-white arms to the bluing dawn and noisily yawns.

"I don't have time for dramatics, Diana," I tell her. "We can't just sit here and wait for the enemy troops to arrive."

She smiles. "How sweet, you're worried about me."

"No, I'm worried about myself. Stump told me the last man that helped you escape Rebellion died suffering. I don't have time for that."

"Okay, I'm ready." She leaps off the rock and starts running down a well-used pathway carved out by many a travelers' feet.

"Wait up! I need to check my compass to make sure we're going in the right direction!" But she's already disappeared in the forest.

I pity the man that marries Diana.

We must be a kilometer from the coastline. The map Benjamin gave me required the use of a compass. We'd veered off the correct pathway to find shelter for the night, so now we had to make a correction or we could possibly not reach Jamestown by sunset.

I found Diana sitting by a blueberry bush, gorging on its berries. Huffing and puffing, I called out, "Save me some, please!"

"Slowpoke."

We rested while I explained how Benjamin's map worked. Diana agreed to be a good girl and not run off again. About that time, we heard a rustling and shouts of angry men, "Over there! I see them."

Diana grabs me by the hand and pulls me toward a cliff.

No, no, no . . . resounds in my skull.

"I know!" She glances back. "We have no other option."

Before I know it, we are leaping to our deaths. The metal box in my backpack weights me down but Diana helps me carry it as we swim in the roiling water rapids. Good thing I know how to swim, but Diana proves to be a champion at the art of survival. We reach the other side of the river and crawl onto the rocky soil of the bank.

Exhausted, I roll over on my back to catch my breath.

She sits up and laughs.

"What's so funny?"

"You're a creampuff! That surprises me."

I am no match for this clever girl.

"What happened to you following my lead?" I sit up, panting.

"No time to think when on the run," she replies, the shadow of her ample breasts pressing against the wet fabric of her thin shirt.

No time to be tempted, I hear the shouts of the men standing at the top of the rocky cliff while searching the river for us. They are furious at being outplayed by Diana. I take no credit for cliff-jumping.

"While I catch my breath, Diana, I have a question."

"Yeah, what?" She stands and shakes her body to dry.

"I spied a huge building on the beach as I left Rebellion—what was it?" I look up at the Amazon lady for a response.

"Oh, that—it's a condensation plant. When rain didn't fall the next year after no one volunteered to make the journey to Jerusalem, our City Council voted to find a way to get fresh water to our village."

"From salty ocean water?" I blink. "Clever."

"Yes, we are, very." She started jumping in place.

"What are you doing?" I rise to my feet, a bit wobbly.

"Preparing to run," she said. "Look!"

I follow the direction of her pointed finger. Several men from Rebellion have found their way around the cliff and spotted us on the shoreline. The last thing I want is to spend Sunday with them.

"I'll lead. You follow," I tell Diana.

We run fast. Eventually, we find the right path that will take us to Jamestown. Forget going different directions at the fork in the road; we're way past that junction. Diana is coming with me.

Benjamin is not going to be happy about the situation.  I certainly am not.  We eventually arrive at the beach and glance around. There is no place for us to hide in the open. We walk for hours until we finally spy Jamestown in the distance and rejoice.  To me, it feels like home.

The sun has already set and the day is cooler.

"Why are we stopping now?" Diana spies the village not far away.

"Gates will soon be closed for the night."  I spread out a blanket on the sand and nearly trip into my bed for the night.

She glares while sassily tapping a foot.

"What is it, Diana?" I am in no mood for her defiance.

"I don't have a blanket."

I glare up at her. "It isn't big enough for two."

"Then let me sleep on it."

*Really?*  I sit up and shake my head.

"You owe me.  I saved your life from my buddies."

"Oh, the cliff." I rise from my bed. "Okay, you get the blanket. I'll just find a nice soft rock farther inland." I start walking.

"Wait!"

I spin around.  "Anything else I can do for you, Diana?"

She scoots to one side of the blanket. "I'm not selfish like you, David," she wittingly remarks. "You can share *my* blanket."

Somehow, it feels like I've been outwitted.

# 10

## Sunday

**"WHO'S THAT GIRL?" BENJAMIN** points to Diana as she climbs upon the deck of his boat, his gaze slipping to the metal canister I carry.

"Diana—I don't know her last name."

"Solomon," she replies, hopping aboard.

Both Benjamin and I do a double-take.

"That's a Jewish name!" our statements collide.

"My great-grandmother was a Jew—a descendant of the tribe of Zadok, the first priest that served in the Mosaic Temple."

I am dumbfounded at what lies this girl can come up with.

"I'm not lying, David.  I see your distrust."

"Okay, kids, let's not argue over the point—I need to get my part to the ship or we'll spend winter here."  He releases the anchor.

"What ship?" Diana and I simultaneously inquire.

"Mine.  Down the shoreline. That way."  He points north.

Today appears to be another day of surprises.

The fishing boat rocks as we set sail along the coastline.  It is a beautiful summer day. Benjamin is at the helm, a pro at sailing. He seems as contented as a bull munching on a tall field of grass.  Me, my stomach hurts as I sit with Diana on the deck.

"Why didn't you tell me you were Jewish?" I ask.

"It wasn't necessary," she replies.

"Expedient, you mean."  I feel a bit betrayed.

"That, too."

Silence seems to satisfy us both.  I don't want to argue with Diana. Obviously, she intends to sail with us to Israel, seeing she claims to be Jewish. I don't know if she's lying or not.  Maybe her parents really were Christian missionaries. Let Benjamin work out the details with her. It's none of my business. I am engaged to Dahlia.  Taken.

The ship in the distance looks like it belongs to a pirate.

"You own this ship?" I query Benjamin as I unsteadily stand up.

"Sailed here in it.  Will sail back in it."

"All the way to Israel?"

"Ya, boy, we'll sail ta' port of Guinea-Bissau, winter ther'."

"But it's only July," I protest. "How long will our trip take?"

"Long as it takes—can't order the weather to obey."

"No, I guess not." *That is Jesus' job.*

"Come spring, we'll sail up the coast to a port in Morocco. Hang out there a week or so, then sail the Mediterranean Sea to Port Polermeo on the tip of Italy. After resting and reloading new supplies, we'll make our way to Israel. Finally, I'll be home ta' see my fam'ly."

Tears press against the back of my eyes, but I won't release them. I miss Dahlia terribly. No way to get word to her by letter. On the other hand, Diana is oblivious to stress, stretched out on the deck like a diva soaking in the warm sunlight to improve her already golden tan. She rolls over and suspiciously glares at me with those magical eyes.

"You don't have to stare, David!"

"I wasn't." I'd only sneaked a look.

"You were the one who set the rules."

*Oh, yeah, the touchy-feely ones*, I recall.

As we approach the shoreline, Benjamin hops out of the fishing boat and grabs the rope at the helm, pulling us inland. Three hearty sailors take over and drag the boat deeper onto the wet sandy beach.

We get off the boat. Gratefully, my land legs work better on land. Before I know it, Diana is racing down the sandy beach, hands waving in the air like a child in a candy shop, nothing forbidden.

"What's she doin'?" Benjamin turns to me.

"I have no idea."

"Why did' ja bring 'er with ya?"

"She somehow escaped Rebellion and followed me," I reply. "Actually, she saved my life at least once. She's pretty athletic."

"So, I see . . ." *hmmm.*

"What is the hmmm for?" I ask.

"Bringin' her with us might be a probl'm," Benjamin whispers. "Some of these sailors hav' not yet become Christians."

"You think they might hurt her?" I wonder if I should tell him that Diana was a Temple Prostitute in the worship of Baal?

"Rape her," he replies. "Or . . ."

"Or what?" I don't like the way this conversation is headed.

"Or you can mar'ry her. Sailors 'll honor that."

I can think of a dozen reasons why that won't happen.

"Or, we kin leav' her here on the shoreline to fend for herself."

"Diana doesn't know anyone here," I point out.

"The Village Elders pro'bly send her back to Rebellion."

"They can't do that. They'll sacrifice her to Baal."

Benjamin's jaw is set, his dark eyes diamond hard.

"What tis it you're not tellin' me, son?"

I bite the bullet. "Diana's a Temple Prostitute."

"A pagan? Who does she wor'ship?"

"Her people worship many idols," I reply. "Baal is the main one because he is the god of weather. It hasn't rained there in fifty years."

"Tha's 'cause the village won't send an envoy to Jerusalem to pay homage to Jesus. No rain is a penal'ty for failing to do so."

*Zechariah 14:18*, I recall the Bible scripture.

"So . . . David! What 're we do'in with Diana?"

My mouth hangs open with indecision.

"Ya 'll marry the girl and mak' the journey," Benjamin declares.

I am sick to my stomach when I think of Dahlia, waiting for me at home while I marry another. I will not consummate the marriage. I will have it annulled before I begin my journey back across the ocean.

The ceremony is performed by Benjamin at sunset. Besides a boat captain, he's a priestly descendant of Amos. I'm the only one without the right credentials to enter Jerusalem. I don't like agreeing to "better or worse," but it's part of the promises a groom makes to his bride.

One thing I know for sure, no bride in the world is more beautiful. I could fall madly in love with Diana—except for Dahlia. But I take our promise to marry serious. Yet, here I am wedding another.

The entire service takes no more than fifteen minutes. A celebration follows. Cookies and ale. Diana dances with each of the sailors. She's happy while I'm trapped in depression.

"Com' on!" Benjamin pats me on the back. "Ya' did the right thing. Saved this girl's life. Jesus honors that."

I nod, thinking he is right, but still . . .

The sails come up at midnight as we are on our way. Diana and I will spend our first wedded night in the captain's cabin. The bed is narrow and hard, but I face the wall as she snuggles up next to me.

Even the rocking ship does not make me sleepy.

"David, it will all work out, I promise."

I am too despondent to answer her.

"I already love you," Diana says. "And I am with child."

I roll over and shove her out of bed. She hits the floor with a thud. "What did you just say?" I am on my feet with rage.

"Don't hit me!" She holds up a defensive hand.

"Be quiet!" I help her to her feet.

"I was supposed to take some awful tasting herb right after my period two months ago. I didn't. I don't know who the father is."

I sit down on the bed and plant my head between two knees. If this night gets any worse, just throw me overboard. I'm not a Jonah, so I have no expectation of a huge fish swallowing me and saving me.

"I'm sorry." Diana kneels in front of me. "If the Baal priests found out, they would sacrifice me and my baby over the firepit."

I grab her hands and we stand together.

"I'm sorry," she says as tears cloud her lovely eyes.

"Sorry doesn't make me feel any better."

"I don't mean to be trouble. I just wanted to leave Rebellion any way I could get out. When you arrived, I saw my way clear."

I nod. "Okay, we'll make the best of this trip."

"Thank you." She smiles sweetly.

But we sailed into a storm before morning and I thought we might die. I've never prayed so hard, promising God I'd help Diana the best I could. But we could not be man and wife. Because of Dahlia.

# 11

## Three Days Later

**WE SAILED THROUGH THREE** storms before the ocean calmed and the ship sails went up again. Diana was sick and threw up early every morning. Benjamin noticed. I had to tell him.

"Diana's pregnant. It's not mine."

He nodded. "No time. You were only gone three days."

I nod. "I'll claim her as my wife, but won't have sex with her."

Benjamin chuckles. "I 'spect that won't be easy."

"I am betrothed to Dahlia. She's waiting for me back home," I explain. "We'll marry when I get back. I can't go back on my promise."

*Hmmm* . . . Benjamin's bearded face reflects doubt.

"You don't think she's waiting for me," I conclude.

"Might be years 'fore you return, son. By that time, you'll be a father, like it or not. You gonna walk away from a child?"

"I—" I never thought of that and the idea disturbs me.

"Sorry to bring up a prob'lem, just sayin'."

We hear footfalls on the deck and turn around.

"How much did you hear, Diana?"

"Enough, David." She's frowning.

I walk over and grasp her hands. "I promise to treat you right, and I'll make sure you and your daughter are safe when I leave."

"What if I have a son?" Her gaze encompasses a lot.

"Either way," I say. "We'll find you a good home."

She nods, turns, and leaves me to finish my conversation with Benjamin. He's smiling as I turn around. "Well . . ."

"I don't want to talk about it anymore."

* * *

The days stretch into weeks, but finally after three months, the ship pulls into Port Guinea-Bissau. Already late October, and farther north than our departure port in Brazil, the weather has turned cold and blustery. I long for the seasonally warm weather back home.

Diana is already showing.  Her appetite is ferocious and she no longer flouts a slender waistline.  But she seems happy to be pregnant and keeps her mouth shut most of the time—except when she thinks I need a talking to—a fussing at.  I refuse to take her bait.

Benjamin, Diana, and I leave the ship to the sailors to batten down for the winter.  Like sheep, Diana and I follow our shepherd.

Bissau is the name of the village where we find shelter in an old inn built a hundred years before.  Only one room with double beds is available, so Benjamin offers it to us. That is, me and Diana.

"Where will you stay?" I ask our captain.

"I won't be far—if ya need me.  The innkeeper will sen' someone to fetch me," he says.  "And if ya need a midwife, we kin find one."

"I don't," Diana says, "I'm not due for three more months."

Benjamin leaves the inn as I receive our room key.  "You ready to go up?" I ask Diana.  She nods and we mount the stairs together.

Our room is quite nice—as inns go.  The mattresses on the beds are comfortable and there are adequate quilts for cover on cold nights.

If I know Diana, she'll crawl in bed with me to keep warm.

Actually, I'm getting used to the idea of having someone to look after. My father always looked after me, but all I ever did in the past was think about myself and my future.  I never dreamed my trip to the City of Lights would turn out like this.  The future is blind, it seems.

Supper is served in the dining room downstairs at six p.m.

The innkeeper's wife cooked and did a fine job with the chicken and late garden vegetables.  A huge fire leaps from a fireplace half the size of one wall. Diana and I are both hungry and eat all we can hold. Alcoholic ale is offered but we turn it down for different reasons.

At our table sits five other travelers on their way to Jerusalem to pay homage to King Jesus. One man is from the Continent of Africa, a small village in Angola. I didn't speak his language, or him mine, but his smile and enthusiasm for the table conversation shows through.

Two women, Catholic nuns from different villages in Argentina, are traveling together. They speak several languages, including an African dialect our friend from Angola recognizes. It appears that God has brought us together to share our different life stories and the reasons why we are on our journeys to meet Christ Jesus in person.

The fourth traveler seated at our table is both deaf and blind. He's accompanied by an elderly female nanny with a flock of gray hair and eyes as blue as cornflowers. Her face is crinkled like a page from an ancient manuscript. I clear my throat to gain everyone's attention.

"Excuse me!" I point to Claudia, the nanny. "Will you tell us more about the young man you're traveling with?"

"Yes, please do," says Beverly, the younger nun.

"Oh, yes. This is Charles. His parents drown in a boating accident when he was ten. I heard about his situation and took him in."

"You adopted him," the second nun Julia says.

"Yes. The boy had no family relatives."

"Very kind of you," I utter.

"Where are you from, Claudia?" Diana inquires.

"The island of Cuba."

"*Cuba?* Isn't it too cold to live there year around?" I erupt.

"Not anymore. Heat is generated from burning coal. Our village has a huge furnace with pipes to our individual homes," she explains.

"Where do you get your coal?" Beverly asks.

"A boat brings it in from America—West Virginia."

"What about vegetation on the island?" Diana asks.

"We are like a jungle. The island was wiped clean by hurricanes and floods prior to the return of Jesus," Claudia says. "But we have a lot of rain on the island now for growing vegetation and certain foods. We have cattle, sheep, goats, and some wild animals as a food source."

"So . . . how did your people survive when the north pole shifted?"

During the seven years of tribulation following the "rapture" of Christ's church on earth, Diana knew that God had cursed the earth. Seasons changed. The land weakened and collapsed. Disease broke out and millions of people died as a result of God's harsh judgment.

Yet, Christianity somehow thrived. It was said back then, "Mercy reigns," by many converts. Many trusted in the name of Jesus.

"Originally, I lived in north Florida with my family," Claudia reports. "After they passed, I moved to Cuba, where my grandparents were born and grew up. The island enjoys sunlight and south winds."

"So . . ." Diana concludes, "because it was warmer there."

Claudia's deep-set brown eyes mist. "Cuba's our home now."

"Yours and Charles," I clarify.

"Yes." Claudia smiles. "Charles saved me."

"I presume that discussion is for another night," Beverly remarks, widely yawning. "I'm too weary from my day to talk anymore."

We finish our meal and separate to our respective quarters. There's a lock and key to our room so I secure it. Diana falls into bed and sleeps instantly. I help her get under the covers, fully dressed.

Me, I'm not sleepy. Maybe a bit concerned about becoming a surrogate daddy to a newborn. Diana is heavy with child, so I wonder if her delivery date will come sooner than expected. Time will tell.

Deep in prayer, I stand at the glassed-in window overlooking the street below, a dull light seeping from burning oil lamps. It's apparent that Bissau offers more life comforts than my home village. Main streets are stone-paved and, like Rebellion, a condensation plant converts the salty ocean into pure water. We have an indoor privy. No need to lurk in the dark on cold nights to relieve ourselves.

With that thought in mind, I crawl into bed, close my eyes and pray: *Dear Jesus, I love you. Help me be the Christian you desire as I make this long journey to see you. And help Diana to know you.*

# 12

# December 24

**SOMEHOW, THE EARTH TURNED** during the night and morning arrives. I wake up to singing outside our bedroom window. It is December 24th, Christmas Eve. My thoughts turn toward home.

Dahlia would be up and dressed by now, helping her mother to prepare for a special celebration tonight in honor of King Jesus. According to Christian tradition, God's Son was born on this date, wrapped in swaddling clothes, and placed in an animal manger. Bethlehem inns were full so Mary gave birth to our Savior in a cave.

Fast forward two-thousand years plus, and Jesus removed His Church on a December 24th. The next seven years were hell on earth.

"Who's singing?"

I felt Diana standing by me before she spoke.

"A young choir of children are in the street," I reply.

"Ring the Bells of Christmas, right?"

I nod, then turn away from the window. She snags my arm.

"Wait, why are you sad? It's Christmas Eve."

I peer at my unwanted companion. Can she see the sadness imbedded in my gaze? I miss home. I miss Dahlia terribly.

"She's not here. We should make the best of it."

I jerk away. "You can never understand how I feel, Diana."

Her gaze falls to the floor. "I'm sorry, but you've moved on."

I've never wanted to slap anyone like I do Diana right now. It's not her fault I married her. It's mine. I had a choice. I lift her chin so we are locked in a gaze. "You're right, no sadness on Christmas."

She smiles. "Good. We should celebrate!"

We are late for breakfast. Our traveling companions on their way to the City of Lights are laughing and sharing old stories concerning their childhood. Diana and I find our place at the table and listen.

Their joy is contagious. Their stories funny. The innkeeper's wife we know only as Bonnie serves the table with slabs of salty bacon, scrambled eggs with cheese, and biscuits. The coffee is hot and strong.

Antonia, the innkeeper, says a prayer over our meal.

Diana eats like there is no tomorrow. Her figure makes me think of a helium balloon my father once showed me in a picture. It was huge enough to support a basket of people clinging to the base, riding high over the landscape. I laugh at its mental comparison of Diana.

"What's so funny, David?" Claudia the nanny asks.

"Nothing." I shrug, embarrassed at my judgmental attitude of Diana. If she's telling the truth, her pregnancy is a result of rape since she claims to have been forced into ceremonial prostitution.

Diana pipes, "He thinks I look funny." She stands up and pokes out her bulging stomach. I want to crawl under the table. We have never discussed our relationship with anyone at the inn. Certainly, Benjamin is not a gossip. Everyone at the table is snickering.

"I don't think you're funny," I deny her accusation.

"You do!" She pokes me in the chest. Hard.

"Would you excuse us?"

I yank her out of the chair and drag her through the vaulted great room and out the front door. We are fighting each other like cats and dogs when suddenly we are hugging and kissing like impoverished lovers. Before we know it, we've stumbled upstairs and into bed.

We are going at it like animals and I cannot stop myself. The guilt for betraying Dahlia engulfs me but I cannot deny my passion for Diana. We are husband and wife, though we've never consummated our marriage. Until now. And consummating it we do with passion.

When we are spent and lying face up on the small twin bed, I hear Diana laugh. She turns over to confront me. "What was that?"

I get up, naked and embarrassed. "A mistake."

"No, you are denying the obvious." She pulls on a nightgown.

I look at her, disgusted at myself.

"You love me, David."

"I don't. I am betrothed to another."

She approaches. "No. You are married to me."

*I am married to you.* I let the words sink into my skull.

We spend the rest of the day in the town square where Christmas trees have been erected with burning candles and tinsel decorations. I don't want to talk about what happened this morning. I don't want to think that I've actually fallen in love with Diana, a prostitute.

*What about my annulment? Is it possible now?*

Bonnie is a great cook. She prepares a sumptuous meal for our supper. She invited Benjamin to join us. After everyone has filled their stomachs, we gather around a Christmas tree next to the great stone fireplace and sing Christmas carols. Home-made gifts are exchanged. Diana has scarfs for the ladies and knitted caps for the men. I'm surprised she knows how to do the wifely things, considering she's served as a prostitute in Baal rituals since she was thirteen.

I wonder if I will ever think of her in any other way.

Benjamin asks me to walk him down the street to his inn where most of his sailors have rooms. He smokes to keep warm. It's bitter cold by now, and the clouds suggest a heavy snow is on the way.

"Ya look diff'rent, son," he notes. "Som'in's changed?"

"No, I'm just anxious for spring to come."

"Long winter a'hed of us. How's it go'in with Diana?"

"We're, uh, okay, I guess."

"Na, nah. I kin tell ya're mor' in that. Lovers, right?"

I don't answer him.

"Yo'r silence says a lot."

We part ways in front of the inn.

Diana is in bed asleep when I return to our room. I'm relieved. I am so ashamed of myself for breaking my vow to Dahlia. Benjamin is right. It is going to be a long winter with many temptations.

# 13

**DIANA GAVE BIRTH IN** late January. A midwife delivered her baby. A girl we named Samantha after my grandmother. Everything had changed between us. We were a couple now. And affection was not denied anymore. Diana was skilled in lovemaking and I had no qualms about her sexual techniques. I always came away a satisfied husband.

We sailed away from Bissau in late March as soon as the north winds shifted and Benjamin felt it was safe to continue on our journey. He was as anxious to get home to his family as I was to reach Israel's shoreline. My heart's desire was to view the glistening city of Jerusalem set high on a hill. What would it feel like to step inside the Millennial Temple built the first decade following the destruction of the beautiful Tribulation Temple during the vicious Battle of Armageddon.

We made two stops to replenish the ship's supplies as we sailed east on the Mediterranean Sea. Finally, we pulled into the Port of Tel Aviv-Yafo. It was mid-May by then. Our daughter Samantha was almost four-months old. She was adorable, a miniature copy of Diana—who'd miraculously regained her original figure with little effort. The woman had endless energy attributed to high metabolism.

"We say our gut'byes here, son." Benjamin pats me on the back. "From heer, you 'll make your way south to Cairo, Egypt."

It takes me a moment to digest his statement.

"Oh . . . you thoug't you'd jus' march up a road to Jerusalem, find the temple and go inside—no questions asked?"

"Hurry up, David!" Diana nudges me. "Sam's hungry."

"I don't understand," I tell Benjamin. "Aren't we in Israel?"

"Ya, but the holy highway doesn't start heer."

"David! Sam!" Diana exclaims, perturbed at me for the delay.

"Hush!" I shout at her. "Then why did you bring us here?"

"'Tis my home. I've done my duty." He turns and walks away.

"Wait!" I feel panic creeping in. "I have a wife and baby. I don't know anybody but you. How am I supposed to get to Cairo?"

"David! Our daughter just peed all over me!"

"Diana!" I am nearly screaming. "Hush up, please!"

Benjamin walks backwards, squawking, "Ya 'll figure it out. Go to the International Embassy and ask for he'p. My job's done here."

Diana is bouncing Sam in her arms, angry as a hornet.

"Sorry I screamed at you," I apologize to her.

"We can't just stand here, David."

"I know. We need directions to the Embassy."

A lad walks up to me and looks up. "Need a ride?"

"Yes, thank you."

It is a bumpy wagon ride, but we are too weary to care. Samantha actually falls asleep due to the motion. I soon learn from the boy Liam that the Embassy has many offices in its multi-cultured, four-story modern building. Every country in the world is represented there.

Liam drops us off at a hotel two blocks from the Embassy. I pay him with a gold coin and we check into a room. Diana will stay here while I walk to the Embassy to learn how we will travel to Cairo, Egypt.

It's a beautiful spring afternoon, the sky wrapped in a web of blue hanging over us. The temperature is unseasonably warm for May.

"You'll be safe here." I kiss Diana on the cheek. "Get some rest and I'll be back before sunset." I have no idea what I am doing.

As I exit the hotel and walk to the Embassy, I consider if Diana qualifies to enter the Temple with her jaded background.

But then, mercy reigns.

I am met by a doorman before allowed to go inside the building that houses embassies from all over the world. At first, he speaks to me in Hebrew. I shake my head. He knows English, thank God!

"No problem, where are you coming from?"

"Brazil," I reply. "Do we have a representative in today?"

He nods. "Go inside and take the elevator to the fifth floor."

The building has generated electricity. Tel Aviv is not like any other settlement I've visited. I wish my father could be here to see all the modern conveniences. Inside the building looks like scenes photographed in magazines before the satellites crashed, the earth nearly burned up from nuclear wars and left the landscape desolate. During the first hundred years, the trees and vegetation grew back.

And people learned how to survive with elemental tools.

I find a door with a sign on it: Brazil. I knock and wait for someone to open the door. Soon, I face a middle-aged woman.

"Can I help you?"

"Yes," I reply, cap in hand. "My family needs a ride to Cairo, Egypt. I'm new in the city and don't know my way around."

"Come in and I'll give you a map. What part of Brazil are you from?" She shows me to a chair with a soft seat and I drop in it.

"A basin not far from Angel Falls," I reply.

"What village?"

"Bethel. My people are originally from America, Tennessee."

"Have you been back recently?"

"What do you mean?" I look at her hard. She's wearing a nametag: *Gloria.* And a nice suit. "Isn't Tennessee still frozen over?"

"No, the snow has melted and people are moving back."

I am shocked. I had no idea. "Did the poles shift again?"

She smiles. "King Jesus is bringing everything into balance."

I nod, because her statement is beyond my imagination.

# 14

**I BRING GOOD** news as I return to our hotel room in Tel Aviv.

"I've arranged for us to ride a bus to Cairo, Egypt."

"When?" Diana asks. Samantha is nursing her ample breasts and cooing like a little angel. I'm in love with our daughter.

"Day after tomorrow. We'll have time to explore the city."

Diana yawns. "I'm hungry. Is there a place close where we can buy food?" She lays Sam on the bed, fast asleep from a full tummy.

"It's too late to take Sam out," I note. "She's down for hours."

"You stay with her and I'll go in search for our supper."

"Are you sure?" I debate if it's too dangerous for her to go out alone in the dark. Then, this city is like no other. And likely safe.

"Do I look like I can't take care of myself?"

"No, you are the Amazon Woman, Diana." She never fails to test me. "Is it okay if I worry Sam's mother might not come back?"

She gives me that look and I wither.

"Okay, go shoot us a cow or something and bring me some grub." I walk over and open the door. "I'll be here when you get back."

"You better!" she huffs.

I hear Diana's footfalls on the floor outside the door fading. I lift a prayer for the poor guy that tries to assault her. Then check on Sam, asleep on the bed with her pug nose stuck up in the air like Diana. She's the queen of this family—which makes me curious about the identity of the *"Prince"* mentioned in the O. T. book of Ezekiel.

I get my Bible from my backpack and turn to chapter 34, verse 23, and begin reading: *"I will establish one shepherd over them, and he shall feed them—My servant David. He shall feed them and be their shepherd. And I, the* LORD, *will be their God, and My servant David a prince among them. I, the* LORD, *have spoken."* Since King David is already dead, this scripture passage refers to a future time when Jesus Christ will shepherd Israel.

Ezekiel reports in the following verses that God will make a covenant of peace with the Jews so they may live securely in the land without fear of dangerous animals. He promises "showers of blessing." Trees of the field will yield fruit and land produce crops. Citizens of the Promised Land will feel safe. No other nation will offer insults to them since the "House of Israel" is God's. He call it MY FLOCK.

Isaiah 62:12 states: *"They will be called a Holy People, the Lord's Redeemed; and you will be called Cared For, a city not deserted."*

When Jesus stepped down on the Mount of Olives and defeated the incarnate Satan's armies against Jerusalem, He established a kingdom rule for the next one-thousand years. The existing temple built during the seven years of tribulation upon earth had been destroyed, so Jesus ordered a new Millennial Temple to be built.

Jesus came through the East Gate of the Temple and entered a room where He would receive world visitors. Jeremiah 3:17-18 states, *"At that time Jerusalem will be called The Lord's Throne, and all nations will be gathered to it, to the name of the LORD of Jerusalem. They will cease to follow the stubbornness of their evil hearts. In those days the house of Judah will join with the house of Israel, and they will come together from the land of the north to the land I have given your ancestors."* David closed his Bible.

Sleepily, he stumbles to the bed and snuggles next to his daughter. Prayers for safety suffuses his thoughts as a dead sleep swamps over him like a silent tsunami. He never heard Diana return to the room with food. She had not yet told him, but she was with child again.

# 15

**IT'S A MONDAY MORNING,** and the city is bustling with activity. There is a herd of people milling through the Tel Aviv Bus Station. The buses are numbered to match our tickets to Cairo. I tell Diana to rest on a bench with Sam and our luggage until I locate our ride.

After checking the numbers of twenty buses, I locate # 28. Which tells me that many people travel through the city on their way to other destinations. An elderly woman with white hair waves at me.

"David! Over here!" she calls out above the din of conversations.

As I walk her way, I recognize Claudia.

"Where is Diana and Sam?" she asks before I can speak.

"I told her to wait on a bench. Where's Charles?"

Claudia draws in a breath. "He didn't make it."

I picture the blind and deaf man accompanying Claudia.

"What do you mean?" I ask.

"Charles took ill on the ship over and passed." Tears cloud her eyes. "I prayed hard over him, but it wasn't God's will for him to live."

I draw Claudia to me, a petite woman. "He will rise again at the end of the millennium," I say. "His reward will be great."

She shakes her head. "I know . . . but I miss him terribly."

"He's given you a reason to survive—you said it yourself."

"So, I have." Claudia smiles. "Are you on Bus # 28?"

"We are." I wave our tickets. "Did you see the driver yet?"

"Was about to look for him when I spied you."

"Let's see if he's already on board." I grasp her hand and we walk to the ascending stairs at the foot of the open door of the bus.

"Hey, mister? When do we depart?"

"Twenty minutes. Better get your gear in the storage bin. Time waits for no man, and I don't either." He chuckles.

Claudia walks with me back to the bench where I left Diana with our suitcases. Only she isn't seated there anymore. A crowd presses around us and I have no idea where to look for her.

"Go back to the bus and tell the driver to wait," I tell Claudia.

"You better find Diana and hurry.  Less than fifteen minutes left before the bus pulls out.  I don't expect that driver to wait."

Now I'm worried.  Where is Diana and Sam?  What if we miss our ride?  Will I have to pay again for three passengers to Cairo?

"Why don't you go back to the bus and insist the driver wait for us while I check inside the terminal and see if your family's there?"

"Are you, uh, sure?" I stutter.

Claudia throws a hand. "Whatever is God's will be mine, David. I'll catch another bus with Diana if we're left behind. Go!  Hurry!"

I waste a moment contemplating Claudia's kind offer.

"Go, David!  I'll find Diana and the pup.  God is good!"

I turn and push my way back through the traffic, praying Diana and Sam aren't in any trouble. When I reach the bus, she's standing there."  I grab her so hard, she almost drops Sam.  "Thank God!"

"What's wrong?"

"Claudia is at the terminal looking for you," I tell her, wanting to shake her.  "I told you to wait on the bench!"  I nearly scream.

"All aboard!" the driver announces.  "Departing in five minutes."

"You are not my keeper, David.  I think for myself."

I mew, "So it seems," below my ragged breath.  "Get on the bus!"

I pause to speak to the driver.  "Will you wait for my friend?  She did me a favor while I came here to look for my wife."

"Sorry, son. I have a schedule to keep."

Diana and I find seats all the way to the back.  I am huffing and puffing, dealing with a wave of anger that is growing.  My wife's lack of respect for me may well cause Claudia to miss this bus.

"Don't be mad at me, David. After you left, I spied a large map of the station posted on a billboard.  I came straight here to find you, seeing time was short till departure.  Our luggage is in the bin."

*She thinks of everything.*

I grasp the backseat in front of me and try to catch my breath. I'm hypo-ventilating. I've read about it in old sports magazine my grandfather collected.  As the bus doors close, I stand up to see if Claudia has made it back in time.  I can't see her anywhere.  It's our fault. We've made her miss her paid ride. No, it's my fault.

"Are you okay, David?"

Slumping down in the seat, I slow my breath and pray: *Dear God, take care of Claudia. Thank you that Diana and Sam are here and safe. Help me to have more faith that you are with us on this journey to worship.*

* * *

"Wake up, David!"

I feel a hand nudge me.

"Uh . . ." I sluggishly open my eyes. "Where are we?"

"A rest stop," Diana replies. "You've been asleep for two hours."

"I have?" The last thing I remembered was closing my eyes and praying. The doors are open and people are exiting the bus.

"I'm getting off, David. Sam needs her diaper changed and I need to use the privy." She climbs over me and heads up the aisle.

I am so sleepy I could lay my head back and return to no dreams. I know that God heard my prayer, and that Claudia will be fine. She has a lot of faith in God's leading. Besides, she's still grieving over the death of the blind and deaf man in her care. So, maybe God has her on a new adventure to find happiness. I pray that it is so.

The bus is empty by the time I step down on concrete.

A desert setting surrounds the oasis. Great sand dunes rise toward the east, soon to shift with the wind patterns. I'm reminded that Egypt is one of the oldest world civilizations. Moses once took his family to the Pharoah to seek shelter during a time when a famine affected much of the Middle East. Before the Battle of Armageddon, Great Pyramids stood outside Cairo with their ancestors buried deep inside.

"David!" I hear someone calling my name.

Spinning around in circles, I spy Julia, the eldest nun from Australia. She is hurrying toward me. "Where is Diana?"

"Inside the building," I reply. "Is Beverly with you?"

"Yes, she's also inside, using the privy and getting refreshments for us." Julia hugs me like I'm her long-lost son. "Good to see you."

"You, too." I wonder why God keeps putting us together. Our crew that spent the winter together at the inn in Bissau.

"Let's go inside and find Bev. She'll be delighted to see you."

"How was your ship ride over? We had a good sail."

As we walk, I share our experience with Benjamin, how he abandoned us at the dock in Tel Aviv. "A boy, Liam, showed up to ferry us to a hotel in his wagon driven by two half-dead horses."

Beverly laughs. "Yes, God is always in the details of our lives."

"There's my wife!" I point to the line forming at the food stand.

"And Beverly's standing right beside her. They've already found one another." Julia's joy is contagious and I feel it pouring over me.

Yes, God has a destiny for each of us. Sometimes it's singular. Sometimes it involves family. Sometimes, God includes friends.

# 16

**EVERYONE IS ON THE** bus again, heading south toward Cairo. Diana is not feeling well. Something she ate had given her nausea. I am not surprised, considering her moodiness the last couple of days.

Hours pass as the bus bumps along the road. Half dozing, I recall a passage in Exodus 13:17. We're on that same route mentioned in the Bible. Historically, the International Coastal Highway was the principal highway carrying traffic between Egypt and Mesopotamia. North of Damascus, the route followed the arch of the Fertile Crescent fed by the Tigris and the Euphrates Rivers that regularly flooded the region.

Once in Palestine, the northern route twisted through the hills and valleys of Galilee all the way to the Mediterranean coastline. The Fertile Crescent supplied prosperity for what is now southern Iraq, Syria, Lebanon, Jordan, Palestine, Israel, Egypt, and parts of Turkey and Iran.

Diana won't even look at me. She's mad and I don't know why. I'm grateful the movement has put Samantha to sleep again.

The nuns, Beverly and Julia, are seated behind us. They have not stopped jabbering about what to expect when we reach Cairo and prepare for our journey north again on the Highway of Holiness. No sinner travels on that route, we've heard. I'm not sure what that means.

*Will there be a committee to judge us, to see if we're deemed holy?*

It's my understanding of the scriptures that Jesus provided the ultimate blood sacrifice for our sins, so what else is required?

Diana has fallen asleep with Sam cooing on one shoulder. Our daughter is a happy soul, always watching others, giggling, and learning. She will probably walk by the time she's a year old. Diana has breastfed her, so she's vibrant and healthy. A beautiful perfect little girl.

I am getting used to being a daddy. But I know the time will come when I must go home and face Dahlia. In some ways, I hope she has given up on waiting for me. Fallen in love and planned to marry. I have done her a great injustice by asking her to wait for me. I pray that King Jesus won't hold that against me and deny me entrance to the Holy Highway. My whole life, I've wanted to kneel before the King.

Prior to the return of Jesus, most of the population in this area were Islam and embraced Muhammad as their Savior. As the Bible foretold, the Egyptian government is at peace with all other nations in the Middle East. Like most citizens of Rebellion, some reject Jesus as their Savior and King. He still honors mankind's freewill to choose.

Time seems to stand still as I nod off to sleep. The next thing I know, Diana's nudge startles me as the bus bumps and stops.

"What is it?" I alert to a problem.

"Time to get off, David. Carry Sam for me?"

"Uh, of course." I lift the limp little girl from Diana's shoulder and cradle her on my own as Diana grabs Sam's diaper bag.

Sounds awaken as people get out of their seats and move to the front exit. We amble down the aisle, following the person in front of us. Outside, I hear clapping and shouts. We are finally in Cairo.

The atmosphere is not what I expected. A welcoming committee is there to greet our bus. We are given water and a snack before a guide instructs us to board a tram that will take us into the heart of Cairo.

I'm surprised the city is so modern. Gasoline powers the train as we zoom along a metal track shooting fire. I wish that my father could see the sights I behold. The scene unfolding is breathtaking.

At another station, we exit the train and board a bus. Our tour guide points out historical sites of interest as we ride. After unloading, we enter a six-story hotel constructed of stone. The hotel entrance is a colorful marble. And inside the building the floors are carpeted.

We stay together as a group and follow our guide to a desk where we each register and receive our room number. We're informed that a banquet will be held for our group this evening. The invitation is printed in several languages. Diana and I are speechless at the sights.

Sam is fussy now and hungry, so we do not tarry riding the elevator up to our room. Once inside our quarters, Diana heads for the bathroom and throws up. I stand there watching her.

"Do you need to see a doctor?"

She stands up and turns around, irritation mounting.

"Go ahead! What did I say wrong this time?"

"How can you be so stupid, David?"

*What?* I have no clue what she means.

"Did I miss something?  Are you ill?"

"No, David!  I know what's wrong with me."

I sit on the edge of a white ceramic tub as water pours from a silver spicket to fill it.  "Okay, why don't you enlighten me?"

"You know.  You're just suppressing the truth."

"What truth?"

"I'm pregnant!" she nearly shouts then cries.

I don't know what to say.  "I thought you knew how to prevent that."  Dumb me. I have no clue how to calm an emotional pregnant female.  "Are you blaming me because you got pregnant?"

Her eyes are shooting arrows at me.

"You think I'm having sex with other men?"

"No, Diana, I didn't mean that."

"I did take the herbs you purchased in Bissau.  They didn't work. I'm pregnant. You're going to be a father. Get used to it."

I am only seventeen years old, yet a full-grown male married to a twenty-one-year-old female who seems always one step ahead of me. I saved Diana's life when I married her before we boarded Benjamin's ship to cross the Atlantic Ocean.  But she ended mine.

Thus, I'm feeling weak and sorry for myself.  I never pictured myself in this position. I'm not sure I'm qualified to handle this situation.  Diana is looking at me like I need to say something.

I don't, but the silence weighs heavy between us.

"Watch Sam, David!  I need to get some air."

She walks out the door and slams it.

I holler back, "Isn't that my line?"

And on target, Samantha starts screaming.

Did Diana feed her?  Is her diaper wet?  Or is she mad, too?

# 17

**DURING THE BANQUET THAT** evening, we learn that visitors to the Millennial Temple can only enter at appointed times. Our teacher quotes Ezekiel 44:9: *"No foreigner, uncircumcised in heart and flesh, may enter the Sanctuary—not even an Israelite."* What about Gentiles?

Didn't Jesus criticize Jewish Christians for demanding that Gentiles be circumcised? Our Savior pointed out that circumcision of the heart was the important issue. As expected, our group has many questions, some of the answers evoking emotional responses.

"So you're calling me a foreigner?" the man from China erupts.

He speaks good English, but not everyone understands him.

"We can't help being foreigners and women!" Nun Julia shoots to her feet. "That rule can't possibly apply to me!"

Nun Claudia pulls Julia down to her chair, embarrassed.

Our host has lost control as mayhem strikes.

"Okay, folks. Calm down and I'll explain," our host shouts.

Diana is not so humble. "Please do! You owe us that!"

I am relieved the hotel offers babysitting. It is already 8 p.m. Egyptian time. If Samantha had come with us, she would be screaming in protest by now in response to the upsetting comments.

"Give me time to explain." The host points to a set of earphones lying on the table in front of guests. The wires to the earphones are attached to a panel with the option to choose a language.

*Very modern*, I discern, praying for understanding. I am certain Jesus has summoned me to Jerusalem to worship Him. Am I required to have circumcision in obedience to the Old Testament prophecy?

Everyone puts on their earphones and selects a language. Now, we are on the same page—like when the Holy Spirit fell upon the Seventy in Jerusalem after Jesus ascended into Heaven. They were confused at first, before all understanding came. This is technology.

"Now, repeat your question, young man," our host says.

Chung Chi does. *Why are we here?*

"Relax, you Gentiles, and our one Jew, Jesus abolished the requirement for circumcision when He walked on earth the first time."

A sigh of relief trickles over our group.

"I'll buy into that," a British woman expresses. "All any of us want is to visit the temple and worship King Jesus."

"That doesn't explain why we are here," I interject.

"Here, you will receive specific instructions regarding the only way you will be allowed to enter Jerusalem, and ultimately the Temple."

"Great!" a woman from Argentina exclaims. "How soon can we receive those instructions and be on our way to the City of Lights."

*Ah*, I think, *Jerusalem must be a bright city, indeed.*

"Sorry, but there will be some delay."

Grumbling erupts among our group.

"Visitations to Jerusalem are limited to certain times of the year, specifically during certain Jewish festivals. You've missed *Pesach.*"

Only one guest present is Hebrew. "The Festival of Unleavened Bread held in Jerusalem on the 15th of Nisan!" he shouts.

"Yes!" our host exclaims. "Which has already occurred this past April eleven. It's too late for you to attend that festival this year."

"So, when we can visit Jerusalem?" I ask, a bit frustrated.

"Your group is scheduled to enter the day before *Rosh Hashanah* begins," the host replies. "In late September."

"What? That's months away!" someone cries out.

The Host hushes everyone with his uplifted palm.

"Trust me, your visit here will be a pleasant experience. Jerusalem is like no other city in the world. Its inhabitants are unique. Prophets of Old walk the streets. You'll learn about Jewish customs and how to conduct yourselves in the presence of King Jesus."

I raise my hand like a clueless school boy.

"Yes?" He recognizes me again. "Your name, son?"

"David," I reply.

"David, you may call me Araya."

"Yes, thank you."

"Your question, David?"

"Is this Hebrew required to be circumcised?"

Some giggle at my question, but I see no humor in it.

"I expect Eli already has been. Right?"

Eli nods. "Right."

"What is required of us?" the Chinaman asks.

"Let's not get into all the details tonight, Chung Chi. I don't want to give your brothers and sisters in Christ a stomach ache before they enjoy a wonderful meal of roast lamb, vegies, and Matzah bread. Those who are brave can sample the bitter vegetables accompanied by *charoset*—a paste made from nuts, apples, pears, and wine. We also have non-alcoholic drinks upon request. Enjoy your evening."

Our host promptly exits the conference room as a young Egyptian woman takes over his role. She leads our group down a flight of stairs to a stunning ballroom with glittering chandeliers swinging over the long tables laden with white tablecloths and sparkling silverware.

I've only seen such sites pictured in old magazines, then realize I came from poverty. How many cities have recovered from the war and become modernized? I suspect wealth and plentiful foods have created problems for some people who want to control others.

When we are seated, an Israelite priest pronounces a blessing over our food, then explains what each food represents according to Jewish tradition. All of this is new to me. But I am excited to learn.

"This is amazing!" Diana's gaze is forged with excitement.

"Are you feeling better tonight?" I inquire as I snap a cloth napkin over my lap like the lady seated next to me does.

"Yes, I only get morning sickness, thank God!" Diana grins.

"Do you know when you're due to give birth?"

Diana's face reddens. "Not here, David. We'll talk later."

The dinner runs late, so by the time Diana and I return to our hotel room, we are wiped out and too tired to talk about her pregnancy. She falls asleep immediately while I, on the other hand, sit in despair.

*Lord Jesus, why did my life turn out like this?*

But I hear no answer. Since a young boy, all I've ever tried to do is serve the Lord in a new world recovering from devastation. I had my future planned out. I would travel to Jerusalem to worship King Jesus then return to my village and marry Dahlia. I would be a good father and husband to her. But that's not going to happen now. I have a wife I don't want, a baby that's not mine, and a second on the way.

*Truth be known, I want to run away and hide somewhere.*

The 8th-century Prophet Jonah wanted to run away, too. He did not want to obey Jehovah and preach repentance to the people in Nineveh. They were practicing evil in disobedience to God's commands, and God was about to destroy the city and everyone in it if they did not repent. Jonah was told to go there and warn them.

Jonah even jumped in the Mediterranean Sea, trying to escape his appointed assignment. But a big fish swallowed him, then spit him out on the bank three days later. Finally, Jonah obeyed and the people repented and God withheld His judgement. This is a lesson for me.

*How can I run from God's will?*

# 18

**DAYS BECOME WEEKS AND** weeks turn into months. The time arrives for our group to board a bus and travel to the entrance of the "Holy Highway" where we will eventually get off. This is the end of the line, the beginning of a new journey where only the qualified born-again Christian can walk. Or ride. I'm not sure how I will travel.

*Will I make the journey alone or with my family?*

"What are you thinking, David?"

I glance over at Diana and shake my head.

"Are you worried you won't meet the qualifications?"

"That's a bit judgmental, don't you think?" I snap at Diana.

"Sorry." She bounces Sam on her knee. "She's peed all over herself." This is information I don't care to hear. "I should change her." She gets up and walks to the back of the bus.

I think of Diana's question and wonder if she's worried about her past keeping her out of Jerusalem. She's publicly repented of her sins and been baptized, but I have no way of knowing her heart. Is it truly circumcised and cleansed? Does the Holy Spirit abide in her?

Everyone aboard our bus is anxious to see what happens next. It's only a ten-mile trip to the Holy Highway's gate entrance. Will there be angels there to qualify each of us before we proceed? We've been told that the saints of the Old Testament dwell in Jerusalem. Those murdered during the seven-year-Tribulation also returned with Jesus.

After Jesus descended from Heaven in a cloud of hosts—myriads of angels and transformed humans traveling with Him—He stepped down on the Mount of Olives as He promised His twelve disciples. He walked the path leading down the mountain and entered the Tribulation Temple through the East Gate. He approached the Holy of Holies and entered there where Satan was crouched in despair.

Two archangels accompanied Satan to the Pit of Darkness and locked him up. The False Prophet was found and locked away, too. It is rumored that the barren desert of Iran was burning with lava. The people in Hell can see out but no living person today can see inside.

"David! Hold your daughter!" Diana tells me as she sits down.

I lift Sam high over my head. She's getting heavy, growing fast. She giggles like any normal eight-month-old toddler. "Did you poo-poo?" I smell her clean diaper to make sure she hasn't peed again.

Sam only giggles and squeezes my nose.

With her on my lap, I glance over at Diana. "Are you mad at me? Did I do something to irritate you?"

"No."

She will not look at me. *Troubling.*

"What is it you're not saying, Diana?"

"It isn't important."

"I think it is." *Am I picking an argument with her?*

"Okay!" She turns toward me. "Am I your wife?"

"Shush, Diana!" I erupt, embarrassed.

The people seated in front of us turn around and frown.

"Can this discussion wait until we're off the bus?" I whisper.

But Diana's bent on making a big scene to prove her point.

"Are you going to leave us when we get to Jerusalem?"

That got the attention of the entire busload of folks.

*Is this woman a mind-reader?*

"You never touch me, or make love to me anymore!" she shouts.

My face is crimson. A discussion about our private sex life is taking place all around us. I want to slap Diana.

*Why is she doing this?*

Araya, our host, walks down the aisle toward me.

"Is there a problem back here?" he asks Diana, not me.

"No," I quickly reply. "My pregnant wife is having a bad day!"

"David!' Diana leaps to her feet. "Tell him the truth!"

By this time, the bus driver has become aware there is a dispute occurring and has pulled over to the side of the road and cut the engine. This is a nightmare and I cannot believe it is happening.

"I think it best if you get off the bus, David."

"I didn't do anything," I object.

But Diana is already on her feet and grabbing Sam from me. I have no other option but to follow her off the bus. My voice has left me. I feel like a fool. Diana and I are standing in the desert.

*Alone.* As the bus drives away. The sun beats down on our heads. And Samantha proceeds to cry. And I wish I could die.

No words can describe my anger at Diana. She won't speak either. Just stands there. Sam does all the talking and screaming and crying. Finally, I realize if we stand here much longer, we will become overheated and pass out. We're in trouble. Help isn't coming.

I glance back at the long road we've come over then spy the long road still ahead of us. There is not a soul on the road. Not the sound of a vehicle, or a creature—especially no human.

We are alone. *Lost.*

Finally, Diana speaks. "I'm sorry."

"Great."

We don't make a move.

"We can't stand here, David. We have to do something."

"What?"

"Pray," she replies. "You always said God answers prayer."

I nod. She's right. "Uh, okay." I bow my head.

Sam gets unusually quiet, watching me. Diana bows her head.

"Dear, Jesus. Things are not right between me and Diana," I confess. "I admit I have had thoughts about running away from my family. I am sorry, Lord. I ask you to give us a way out of our awful situation." I pause to reflect on what else I need to say.

I grasp Diana's hand. "I'm sorry, Diana. I have done you an injustice in marrying you. I thought I was saving you from death, but I've felt like I've been dying inside for the past year. I've made a choice and there is no going back now. We are together. We are a family."

Diana is weeping by this time. I hear that small inner voice speaking to me: *"David, you needed to repent of your rebellion against what I have given you—a wife and a daughter. A family. Now, you can continue on your path to Jerusalem and worship me."*

Diana says, "I heard what Jesus told you. Is that true?"

"Yes, Diana." I am weeping. But Sam is laughing, joyously. I think I can hear angels singing somewhere and the desert air smells fresh.

"Look, David!" Diana points.

I turn around and see our bus backing up to pick us up. The door opens and Araya says, "The Lord said to go back and get you."

# 19

**A CLEANSING RAIN FALLS** like twinkling lights alongside the River of Life that flows from the Temple in Jerusalem. Our group walks the trail beside the river for the first half mile. We are all wet, but do not mind. Each raindrop feels like manna to our souls as the LORD cleanses us for our journey. It is so true: Mercy Reigns.

No one speaks. Even Samantha is enthralled with the view all around us. We are in the middle of a desert that blossoms with vegetation alongside the River of Life as it overflows its banks. We have been told that the trees bear natural fruit that is used for medicine to heal sick people of their ailments. I can feel the cleansing as I walk.

The pathway ends and we gather as a group. Our new leader is Jabok, a converted Muslim to "The Way," as he refers to belief in Jesus as Lord and Savior. He is short and stout and has a stern base voice. His skin is dark from the tanning sun but he appears in perfect health.

"Welcome to the Holy Highway," he tells our group. "You will now board a bus and travel north to Jerusalem. Enjoy the views."

I smile at Diana as we hold hands. The sweetness of our relationship has grown since our desert experience when we were abandoned and left alone to fend for ourselves. Jesus needed to make an impression on me that I was wrong to be angry about my circumstances. As we choose, we must live with the consequences.

I can see that Diana has changed toward me now that we are a couple. Even Sam feels our family connection. I now understand why Father God put Adam and Eve together to forge a new family on earth. Males and females need each other to complete a holy union. I know that Dahlia will be disappointed with me when I return home. When *we* return home, for Diana and our two children will accompany me.

After we are seated on the bus, Diana asks, "What have you been thinking about, David?" Her gaze is endearing and respectful.

"Us," I reply. "We are a family now."

Tears drip from her black almond-shaped eyes. "I love you."

"I love you, too," I repeat and mean it.

The scenery along the roadside is breathtaking.  Never were the leaves on the healing trees greener. The fruit is large and different colors.  Twinkling raindrops continue to fall as the temperature of the River of Life heats and vapor rises over its banks to produce rain.

We do not reach the city limits of Jerusalem till late evening. I am amazed at the brightness of the city.  No wonder people call it, the "City of Lights.  It's because the glory of the LORD hovers over it.

Our bus pulls into a station where we all get off.  A guide leads our group to a hotel where we will spend the night.  There is no charge for our room on the second floor. The interior is impressive, very modern, with a large, comfortable bed.  Sam is sleeping so I place her on a blanket on the plush floor carpet. She breathes easily in slumber.

After Diana and I bathe and change into our night clothes, we lay in bed staring up at the glistening-white ceiling. It's been a remarkable day in our lives.  I roll over to face her and we discuss our trip. We both feel like we've been washed clean in holiness and ready to enter the Temple tomorrow, but have no idea what that will be like.

Diana falls asleep as I project my thoughts until I pass out.

# 20

IN ZECHARIAH 8, the prophet states that people will come—residents from many cities, one person from a different city—and say to another, "Let's go at once and plead for the Lord's favor and seek the LORD OF HOSTS!" Many people from strong nations will travel to Jerusalem.

In those days, ten men from nations of every language will grab the robe of a Jewish man tightly and say, "Let us go with you for we have heard that God is with you." This passage of scripture is in my thoughts as Diana, Sam, and I go downstairs to the hotel restaurant for breakfast the next morning. "Did you sleep well?" I ask my wife.

"Marvelous!" she exclaims. "You?"

"Never better." I have Sam in my arms. She giggles and coos, uttering, "Mama, mama . . ."

"Did you hear that, David? She called me Mama."

"Da-da," I say to encourage Sam to call out my name.

"Da-da, da-da, da-da," she babbles and we laugh at her.

Breakfast is self-serve at a long table laden with jugs of papaya, orange, and tomato juices. There is a platter with every imaginable kind of fruit and nuts. The bread is fresh and the butter golden with flavor.

Diana eats heartily, her plate filled with scrambled eggs and slices of baked chicken. She's five months pregnant and will give birth in January. Sam will be a year old when our second is born.

We board our bus at 10 a.m. to travel to the Temple Courtyard entrance. From there, we will walk the rest of the way to the Temple.

From my classes in Cairo, Egypt, I learned when Jesus stepped down on the Mount of Olives upon His return to earth, He split the land from west to east. Jerusalem was raised higher between two valleys, north and south. It was recorded in the Old Testament.

Our group approaches a series of steps leading up to the Temple. The climb is steep and challenging. While following others, I recall the former Tribulation Temple was destroyed in the Battle of Armageddon waged by Satan against King Jesus. After the dust had settled out, the city recovered and the Millennial Temple was constructed.

Many saints and angels descended from Heaven with Jesus to dwell in Jerusalem. On these premises somewhere walks the Apostle Paul, the Twelve Disciples, even Adam and Eve, and martyred saints.

The Festival of Booths is celebrated by the Jewish people today. It is the last Friday in September, exactly five days after Yom Kippur, or the "Day of Atonement," the holiest day in Jewish tradition. "Sukkot" means Huts or Booths. In the olden days, the huts were erected by the Israelites to celebrate the end of harvesting grapes and summer crops. The celebration is a time of thanksgiving to express appreciation for all the good things God gives to humankind on earth.

Forty minutes later, we arrive at the South Gate to the Temple. Visitors may either enter through the North or South Gates. After angels qualify us, we will go inside and tour the interior. We will each take our turn to kneel before King Jesus and worship Him. Today, the dream of a lifetime has been fulfilled—just to be here and to know that I am redeemed from sin by God's mercy and grace through His Son.

No one speaks a word as we pass through a large portico and enter the Temple. Our guide shows us the rooms where the animal sacrifices are prepared and explains to us that the purpose of the ritual is to fulfill Jewish prophecy in the Old Testament. There are rooms for the singers and musicians and the priests that serve in the Temple. Our God leaves no detail undone. He will complete a good work that He began on earth as recorded in Genesis. I'm overcome with excitement.

Diana is speechless. Sam giggles and points everywhere. I know our daughter cannot understand why we are here or our purpose, but I will teach her later the importance of our visit. Perhaps, our grown daughter will travel to Jerusalem one day. Only time will tell.

Diana glows in the light of the Temple. Her beauty is noted by other visitors. When we have seen the special rooms, we wait for Jesus to summon each of us to Him. Salvation is an individual gift. We will not go inside the chamber where He sits as a family. But Sam will go with me to bow before Jesus and receive His Word for our lives.

Diana's name is called before mine. She lets go of my hand at the last moment before entering the chamber where Jesus sits on a throne.

I pray for her while she is visiting with the Lord. I know she is repenting of her sin of serving the false god, Baal. She's already been forgiven through grace, but she needs to forgive herself. I am confident that Jesus will help her work through all that stress and guilt.

She returns glowing. I now understand why Moses covered his face after facing Jehovah God. You cannot stand before so holy a God without receiving some of the anointed glow surrounding Him. Diana has that glow on her face. She is radiant, beautiful, and cleansed.

It's my time to go before the Lord. The door to the chamber slides open and I enter carrying Samantha. I stumble to my knees in awe of Jesus's majesty as He sits on His throne, smiling at me.

"Give her to me," he says, so I hand over our daughter. I am speechless. The holiness I feel in this room is overwhelming.

Sam plays with Jesus' beard and giggles as He tickles her.

Who am I to experience so great a privilege? After all the danger I've endured, a marriage I did not want, what do I say to Him?

Jesus' eyes are blue, I think. But they seem to change colors as I stare at Him. He looks around thirty and has the rugged hands of a carpenter. His toga glistens white. A golden crown is on His head. I can clearly see the scars where the nails were hammered into his flesh.

"What is your heart's desire, David?" Jesus asks.

I kneel before Him. "To worship You today."

"Surely, you have another request."

I think about what is important to me. Finally, I lift my head and make eye connection. "Will you comfort Dahlia, my betrothed? I know she will be devastated when I return home with my new family."

"Dahlia will be fine, David. She has her own spiritual journey. Don't worry about her. She's mine and I am tenderly watching over all that happens to her. Trust me to take care of her."

"Thank you, Jesus." My head is still bowed.

"As far as this little girl, Samantha will grow into a fine woman. She will be a leader of your village, an example to the next generation. I will bless her with a good husband and many children."

"Thank you, Jesus." I rise to my feet.

*What about my life?* The question lingers in my thoughts.

Jesus inhales deeply. "You've been faithful to Me all of your life, David, so you will grow old in grace, but your way will not be easy."

It hasn't been easy lately, I recall.

"Fear not, I am with you even till the end of time," Jesus says. "Many people who come after you will remember your works."

I don't understand what Jesus means. *Works?* But I trust Him as my Savior.  And I know my life is safe in His strong hands.

"Go in peace, my Child."

With Sam in my arms, I quietly leave the chamber.  As I stand outside the Holy of Holies people stare at me. What do they see?

# 21

**THE LAND IS TERRACED** on the north side of the mountain. The grass is green and the small fruit trees provide shade for the small groups gathering for conversations. Diana and I stand a few moments at the top observing the activities below. Sam wants to get down and crawl, so I let her. She is nine months and will walk soon.

We watch our daughter as she tries to climb down to the next terrace backwards. She loses her balance and tumbles backwards. Surprise is on her small face as she looks up at us and trembles.

"It's okay, Sam," I call out to her. "You're fine. No problem."

She laughs and starts running again.

"We'd better go get her before she hurts herself," Diana says as she springs forward to go after Samantha. I am a step behind.

Diana snags Sam by the arm and hoists her up. "Enough, Sam!"

Sam giggles and fights Diana to get down. Not happening.

As we stand on the second terrace and look up, I can see the Temple is three stories high. I wonder if the Twelve Disciples live on one of those floors. As I turn around, I notice Diana has joined the group below us. I hurry to catch up and find myself facing a very short, stout man with a stern face. Jewish, through and through.

It's Paul of Tarsus, the Apostle that had an encounter with Jesus after His ascension into Heaven. Paul was on the road to Damascus to punish Christians for their false beliefs that Jesus was God's Son. He was struck blind after seeing a great light shining down from Heaven. Jesus spoke to Paul but the others with him didn't understand what was said. Whatever Jesus told Paul changed his thinking. From then on, Paul preached Christ to the Gentiles and many were converted to Christianity. Yet, here he is today: teaching others again.

I collapse on the grass next to Diana to hear what is being taught. Most of Paul's congregation are Jewish men wearing priestly clothes. They have many questions, and Paul has all the answers. Particularly, they want to know what happened to Paul after he received his sight and went into the desert for three years to prepare for his ministry.

Paul laughs. "I didn't feel alone, men. I was never hungry because the animals fed me. At night, I slept unafraid because an angel stood by my side as I lay on hard rock that felt impossibly soft. I read everything I could about The Way, as it was called in those days."

I perceive that this conversation could last for some time. Sam grows restless sitting, so we move farther down the mountainside.

Huts have been erected on the next two flat surfaces. The odor of fresh-baked foods permeate the air and I realize we had not eaten anything since breakfast. I had lost all sense of time.

"Are you hungry?" I ask Diana.

"Sam is. She's gnawing her fingers."

"Let's go inside this hut and see if there is food for sale." I still have gold coins to spend that my father Joseph gave me before I left my village over a year ago. So much as changed since . . .

The wife of the family occupying the hut offers us bread infused with dried fruits, nuts, and honey. I'm reminded of a cake my mother once made for Christmas. The chicken eggs are pickled and delicious.

The priest's wife spoons mashed sweet potato into Sam's small mouth because the bread is too hard for her to chew. She had not yet grown a full set of baby teeth. I eat till I am ashamed of myself.

Diana has no dietary scruples and eats even more.

We join our group at the base of the mountain and follow our guide into the city of Jerusalem where more huts are erected, more stories being told, and more food consumed. Joy is in the air.

We linger in the city for hours, walking the streets until sunset when our guide summons us to the bus. It's a good drive to Tel Aviv.

# 22

**AS WE DRIVE OUT OF** Jerusalem, I quietly observe how courteous people are treating each other.  Then I realize that angels are present in the city.  It's hard to tell the difference between an ordinary human being and an angel just by looking since they are dressed similarly; not until the angel's image fades in and out or disappears. Sam has her nose to the bus window and notices. She laughs and points a finger.

"Don't point!" Diana grabs her small finger. "It's rude, Sam."

"Diana, she doesn't know how to be rude."

I notice a large man wearing a priestly garb as he carries a grocery sack in one arm for an elderly woman as they cross the street together. She turns around to thank the man but he promptly disappears.

"Lookie-lookie!" Sam mutters as she points again.

"Stop it, Samantha!" Diana fusses at her.

"She's still just a baby," I remind my wife.

"No, Sam needs to be disciplined.  She's too much like me."

*Head-strong*, I think, but dare not say.

"Our daughter needs to learn how to act in public," she adds.

"A worthy cause, but rules mean nothing to Sam."  I stretch my arms over my head and shift my bulk, yawning widely.

"How far is it to Tel Aviv, and do we have a room rented?"

"I presume our host has taken care of the details." I yawn again. It is very dark outdoors, but a full moon is due to rise soon.

"Aren't you tired?" I ask Diana.

"No, I feel a bit energized."

"What did you and Jesus talk about?" I inquire.

"Stuff," she replies.  "Too personal to discuss."

"Even with me?" I feign hurt as I place my hand over my heart.

"What did Jesus tell you?" she asks.

"He explained what Heaven was like after His ascension," I reply. "I asked Him about the reward banquet He held for the saints."

"And did you comprehend what it was like?"

"Not really. The Bema Banquet rewarded the saints for their good works on earth—as a bonus." I smile. "His gifts are spiritual."

Diana nods. "The Bible mentions receiving crowns for our good deeds done on earth. I wonder if we'll get a reward banquet."

"I didn't see anything written about it in the Bible, so I don't know. Maybe not. Is that important to you, Diana?"

"Maybe. I like to think my soul is beautiful to Jesus."

"Because physically you are gorgeous."

Diana looks at me, surprised. "You've never said that to me before." There are tears in her gaze. "Thank you." She chuckles.

"What's funny?"

"You are gorgeous, too, David, but you don't know it."

"What is this?" I punch her lightly on the arm. "Is this a reward banquet we're giving each other? Talking about our good qualities?"

"Well, if you want to think about that . . ." she punches me back then whispers, "You are very good in bed, too."

I am actually blushing. "I'll show you what is good when we get to Tel Aviv." My heart fills with love for this woman I used to despise.

Our bus driver announces that we'll arrive in Tel Aviv–Yafo in approximately an hour, considering the curvy roads. Our guide has booked rooms at a hotel near the Yafo Port, also spelled Joppa.

On our way south to Cairo, Egypt, we had bypassed the bustling city famed to be a major economic center in Israel. Situated on the Mediterranean coast sixty kilometers from Jerusalem, Tel Aviv-Yafo was founded in 1909 as a Jewish-garden suburb of the ancient Mediterranean port of Jaffa, now called Yafo. Since the early 21st century, many governmental agencies founded headquartered here, but the Ministry of Defense has little work to do during peaceful times.

"Did you finish reading the pamphlet?" Diana refers to the printed paper I have been looking through for the past fifteen minutes.

"Yes, and I recall that Joppa was a city during Old Testament Bible times." I tri-fold the printout and place in in my shirt pocket.

"Is this a one-night stopover, or will we stay longer?"

"I don't know, Diana." I pat Sam on the back as she burps.

After Israel became a nation in 1948, Tel Aviv grew to become the largest city in Palestine, surpassing the size of Jerusalem. Against Muslim complaints from Palestine leaders, U.S. President Donald Trump moved the American Embassy from Tel Aviv to Jerusalem in

2017. I glance over at Diana and realize she'd heard little I'd said. She was fast asleep and Sam had settled sleepily on her shoulder.

It's after 10 p.m. when we settle down for the night in our hotel room. Sam is awake and cranky—cutting her baby teeth. Diana rubs her gums with a numbing solution we bought at a pharmacy in Jerusalem. Sam calms and falls asleep in my arms as I rock her gently.

I drop my clothes on the floor and literally fall into bed. Diana is already on her side, snoring. I keep wondering how we will manage when our newborn arrives in January. Will we still be in Israel?

As tired as I am, I can't sleep. My mind is too full of thoughts about all that happened inside the Temple today, and later in the terraced northern courtyard. My village friends back home will want a detailed report when we get there. Maybe I should keep a journal.

I rattle though the desk drawers looking for a blank piece of paper or a notepad to use in recording my recollections of today.

"David! What are you doing? I'm trying to sleep!"

"Good for you, I can't, Diana." I turn around in my bare feet and glare at her. "Do you have a blank notebook with you?"

She yawns, ignores me, and turns over in the bed.

"Diana!" I call out, and Sam lets out a squeal.

My beautiful wife is not happy with me. "Now, look what you've done!" She shoots out of bed and grabs Sam off her pallet on the floor. The little girl cannot be calmed. Her gums are screaming again.

"Give her to me—go back to sleep, Diana."

"If I can." She drops wearily in the bed.

"Shuu!" I hush Sam and step out onto the concrete patio.

We are five floors up in the hotel with a great view of the Yafa Port stretched out below. Houses are stacked on the hillside and look like colored ribbons flowing away from the hotel. The moon rises behind us and glistens on the water. Even Sam notices and points.

I draw her small nose to mine. "It's a beautiful, peaceful world you live in, sweetie," I whisper. "I know you don't understand much of what's going on around you, but I'll tell you later. Like my father did me, I'll teach you about King Jesus. You will love our Savior."

We sit together in a molded chair for some time before I feel my body relaxing and Sam falls fast asleep. It's time to go back to bed.

# 23

I **MADE SEVERAL TRIPS** north to the port where I had last seen Benjamin Cohn, the ship captain that brought us to Israel in his sailing vessel. On a sunny day in mid-October, I finally found him preparing to sail west again with his motley crew of young men hungry for adventure. "David!" he waves at me as I approach him.

"Where are you sailing to this time?"

"The Virginia coast in America," he replies.

"Isn't it still frozen over there?"

"Been a recent warmin'," he notes.

"Who are you picking up?" I inquire.

"Takin', son. A couple from Russia are homesteadin'."

"Who's in charge now? I thought D.C. shut down."

"America is reop'in now. New congress in Alabama."

"Is the earth's axis shifting back?"

""Bove my paygrade, son." He glares. "What kin I do fer ya?"

"Diana and I are ready to return to Brazil," I inform him. "Any chance you could veer south and take us back to Jamestown?"

"Winters are tough. Anyhow, booked solid with customers till spring," he says. "Maybe in March, when the ocean shows me favor."

"I've been meaning to ask someone why is it so warm in Israel while the rest of the world is cold during winters."

"Ah . . . tis the presence of the Holy Spirit here that warms the air." He spits. "But the earth is greening ever'wher now, I hear."

I think about Diana's pregnancy and wonder if she's healthy enough to make the trip to Virginia first. "When do you set sail?"

"Tomorr'a' mornin'. Got a cancellation, if ya wanna go."

"No. Diana's pregnant again. She'll give birth in January."

"Congrats, son!" Ben slaps me on the shoulder. "Ship ain't no place for a puny woman. Plus, I wouldn't be sailin' with a wee one till the pup's at least three months old. Best you wait winter out here."

"No choice, I guess." It's settled, we stay in Israel. "How can I find you in March, if everything goes well and we're ready to leave?"

"I'll be stayin' at the Benedict Inn." He points to a street. "Go 'bout a half kilometer—the inn is on your right. Can't miss it."

"Thanks, Ben." I throw a hand and head back to our hotel in Tel Aviv-Yafo. Diana and I will need to look for an apartment, or a house to rent until next spring. By then, I'll be gone from home nearly two years. I wonder what Dahlia is doing? Has she given up on me?'

The trip back takes an hour.

Diana left me a note in our hotel room saying she's taking Sam shopping, be back in a few hours. Our daughter has outgrown her clothes and needs training pants. Now that all is quiet, I sit down at the desk to record my thoughts concerning the past three weeks in my new notebook. My gold coins are nearly gone, so I need to find work.

Two hours later, Diana returns with a sack filled with new clothes for Sam. Our little girl runs into my arms and snuggles.

"Did you have a good day?" I stow my notebook away, not ready for Diana to read my private thoughts. Some of my comments are about our risky relationship. Some she definitely won't like.

"Great! Did you find Benjamin?" Diana asks.

"Yes, he can't take us south to Port Guinea-Bissau till spring."

"Why not?" Diana stows Sam's clothes in a dresser drawer.

"No use putting those clothes away," I say, not answering her question. It seems we are not on the same page this afternoon. "We have to find permanent shelter—an apartment or a house."

Diana stands motionless, questioning how we will manage.

"Maybe the hotel manager knows of someone who can keep Sam while we look for a suitable place," I suggest. "Now, if possible."

"Why the hurry, and why can't Ben take us to Guinea-Bissau?"

This woman pushes me over my last cliff as she sassily parks a hand on one hip. She's a lovely lightning storm when irritated.

"He's sailing to America with other passengers," I reply.

She smacked her lips. "An apartment?"

"Or house. We're almost broke, so I need to look for a job."

"Okay, watch Sam while I track down the manager and find someone to stay with her." She checks the time. "It's nearly 3 p.m."

"I know, so hurry up."

Diana is out the door on a mission.  Sam is chewing on a cherry lollipop and red saliva dribbles down her clean white shirt.

"Ooey, sticky!"  She sucks her fingers.

"Come here." I take her sucker, and lips pucker to cry.

"You can have it back when I wash your mouth, change your shirt, and put a bib on you," I tell her, and she seems to understand.

While I have Sam on the bathroom counter washing her face, she goes limp and falls asleep.  Good!  I place her on the bed for a nap.

Diana is back in thirty minutes with a maid. "Elsa says she can stay with Sam for a few hours.  She brought a snack for her supper."

"Do we have food here for Sam?" I ask.

"Yes, I have a jar of apple sauce and she can have a banana."

"Okay, let's take a walk and see if we can find a rental apartment or a house before sunset."  I glance at Elsa.  "Thank you."

"No problem."

We are out of the hotel on the streets walking by 4 p.m.  It gets dark around 5:30 so that limits our time looking.  "Let's pray."

"Right here in the middle of the street?" Diana is surprised.

"Yes.  Right now." We bow our heads. "Lord Jesus, you know our need for shelter.  Help us find a suitable place where we can spend the next five months.  Amen."  I open my eyes and Diana is weeping.

"What is it, honey?"  I grasp her shoulders and pull her to me.

"You prayed the exact prayer I prayed silently a few minutes ago," she replies.  "Now I know for sure Jesus has heard us and will answer."

And He does.  By five o'clock we are signing to rent the upstairs apartment in a house owned by a priest's widow.  She will let us live there free if Diana will shop for groceries and do the cleaning while I work."  It's the best possible answer to prayer we could get.

By six, we are back at the hotel.  I pay Elsa a gold coin and thank her.  "Anytime, you know how to find me."  She leaves our room.

"Are you hungry?" Diana asks.

"Starving.  Let's go into the city and find a restaurant tonight.  I feel like celebrating.  Maybe Jesus will show me a job while we're there."  I pick up Sam and swing her around.  "Wanna go on a walk?"

"Walk, walk!" she squeals, and off we go to Wonderland.

# 24

## Jupiter, Brazil

**DAHLIA IS HANGING WET** clothes to dry on a line strung between two trees. The autumn wind is brisk and chilly today. Her thoughts are heavy on David. She has not heard from him, if he has successfully reached Jerusalem to worship King Jesus. As far as she knew, no one in Jupiter had received news from overseas, so perhaps getting a letter through was impossible. Not knowing was driving her crazy.

Joseph Goldman stood on a hill outside of Jupiter observing Dahlia. Beautiful and serene as she worked, his news would likely put a frown on that lovely face. Still, she should know what he'd learned from his trip to Jamestown on the Atlantic coast. He approaches from the front so as not to scare her. As if sensing a presence, she pulls back a flapping sheet and glares at him. *David* formed on her lips.

Her word is too far away from him to physically hear, but he's read her lips. Sitting down on a rock, hands folded in her lap, she waits for him to approach. Joseph takes his time. News isn't good.

"Good morning, Dahlia."

"Mr. Goldman," she nearly whispers, anxiety in her expression. She knows he's come concerning David.

"Can we go inside and speak?" He refers to the cottage.

"Sure. It's chilly this morning, so I'll make us some hot tea.

"Thank you." Joseph had walked for two hours and was tired and thirsty. Hot tea sounded perfect to embolden him to speak frankly.

"You've heard from David," she says when indoors.

Joseph follows her into the kitchen and sits at the table.

"No, but I've been to Jamestown and know he made it that far. A sailor that helped load cargo on a ship headed for North Africa in July said he spied a young lad about David's age boarding that ship."

Joseph falls silent, dreading to tell the rest of the story.

"Alone?" she says as if anticipating something awful.

"No, he had a young woman with him."

Dahlia glares a moment, light glinting in her lovely green eyes.

"They appeared to be together," Joseph continues.

"What am I to assume, Mr. Goldman?"

"Nothing, I suppose. I just thought you should know."

"And now you've told me." Dahlia stiffens. "I know David. We are betrothed. If he was with a woman, he's helping her."

"Probably."

"You've had no letters from him?"

"No."

"I will not give up on us," Dahlia confesses. "David will have to come here and tell me himself that we are not to be wed. Otherwise."

"Otherwise, you will wait for his return."

Dahlia nods.

"I just thought you should know."

"And now I do." She turns to resume making the tea.

Feeling like a naysayer, Joseph waits to be served his tea.

They drink the beverages in silence. When he's finished, he places his teacup in the sink. "I should go now."

"Thanks for the report." Dahlia walks him to the door.

Noting Dahlia's distress, he turns around to finish the story. But he doesn't. He won't tell her about David's visit to Rebellion, noted for Baal worship. Or that the girl with David is a temple prostitute.

There is much he doesn't know about that situation.

"Is there something else, Mr. Goldman?"

"No. Thanks for the tea. Have a good day."

Dahlia watches David's father until he disappears in the colorful foliage of the hillside. There's something more to that story.

* * *

### Back in Tel Aviv-Yafo

The sun had long set when David left the hotel with Diana and Sam. Their supper was delicious at a little Middle-eastern café located on the wharf. Again, a full moon made its way over the eastern horizon and set the ripples of the Mediterranean Sea alive with color. Even Sam was joyous over God's marvelous portrait. All was going well. They had a place to live for the winter. Free, with Diana's help.

"So, you'll look for a job tomorrow." Diana licks salt from her fingers. They had the baked cod with sauteed mushrooms and onions.

"I'm good at carpentry. A skilled handyman is always useful at a craft or a blacksmith shop," he says. "Just takes some looking."

"Greta said we could move into our upstairs apartment tomorrow morning," Diana reminds me. "I told her not to clean the apartment, I would." She washes Sam's face with a wet napkin. Our little girl is falling asleep with her head nearly hanging in her messy plate.

"We have to get Sam back to the hotel and to bed." I remove a gold coin from my pocket, one of two left over from my trip. I miss my father and friends. I miss home, but Diana and Sam are my family.

"You look sad," Diana notes as she lifts Sam from the highchair.

"No, just missing my father."

Diana huffs. "You're lucky to have a father to miss."

No comment, I go straight to the cash register to pay our food tab. The Arab woman gives me back change in *agora* currency. There are 100 agoras in one Israeli shekel, or an ILS as it's called. Gold is treasured as a world currency. I suspect the cashier will trade agoras for my coin and take it home to purchase something later.

When the Antichrist ruled over world politics during the seven years of tribulation, people threw their gold coins away as worthless. Only the electronic Mark could purchase goods and services.

Diana was waiting for me outside the restaurant with Sam.

"What took you so long?"

"What's your hurry?" I return.

"Here's your sleepy daughter. You carry her."

And so, we are off to the hotel, hopefully for a quiet night.

# 25

## Christmas Eve

**THE CRAFT SHOP I** work for closes at 4 p.m. on Christmas Eve. Jonathan gave his workers Christmas Day off with pay. I had saved enough agoras in the past nine weeks to pay Benjamin for our trip home in the spring since our rent was free. It's nearly dark in Jaffa.

As I enter a jewelry shop to purchase Diana's gift, doorbells tinkle a welcome. My father once told me the horses in Jerusalem have bells on their collars to remind us of holiness. I know that to be true now.

I am anxious to see Diana's face when she opens my present. Our daughter Samantha is nearly a year old, smart as a whip, and talking up a storm. She's a copy of Diana—beautiful like a whirlwind dancing across the Egyptian desert. I've made a wooden rocking horse for her and Diana has purchased a new pair of shoes for her growing feet.

By now, supper will be on the table waiting for my arrival.

"Good evening, sir. May I help you?"

I glance up at the elderly gentleman behind the jewelry counter. The bright light from the case makes his face shine. He has a beard like Santa Claus pictured in magazines; his eyes, a marble blue. Seeing dimples winking at the corners of his small mouth makes me chuckle.

"I see you are in a good mood!" His bushy gray eyebrows arched. An amusing smile trickles across his plump pink lips.

"I need to buy a wedding ring." I place my bulging canvas purse with agoras on the counter so he can see I mean business.

"A ring, ya! I have quite a selection." He unlocks the counter and removes three. All are beautiful, glittering with light, and expensive.

*Diamonds are a girl's best friend*, one American actress said long ago. *Marilyn Monroe*, I recall the sexy blond starring in old 1950's movies.

"Which one?" he inquires.

It takes some convincing to bargain for the ring I want to give Diana for Christmas. The Jew haggles with me over the price I want to pay. I tell him that is all I have. Sell me the ring or forget it.

He's about to close his shop, so he grumbles at me but sells the ring for the price I want. His wife wraps the ring, grinning the whole time. I think she enjoys that I won the pricing contest. I certainly am.

Christmas trees are standing alongside the street as I hurry home—well, the apartment that Diana and I call home. I can't wait to see her joyful smile when she opens my gift tomorrow morning.

It's dark by now. There's only one lamp glowing in the window of Greta's house as I let myself inside with a key. The tree lights are turned off for the night. The table still set for supper, but no one is there.

I check upstairs to see if Diana and Sam are there.

Where is Greta? I stand alone in the living room puzzled. Am I to wait? Or look for them. As I contemplate the mystery, there's a rap at the front door. I turn around and rush to see who stands there.

It's Greta's friend, Judith. She looks forlorn.

"Did something bad happen?"

"They went to the hospital—Diana's in labor!" Judith gushes.

"Where is Sam?"

"At my house. Gordon is with her."

"What hospital?"

"St. Emanual on Fifth Street. They left an hour ago."

About the time I was finishing up work and leaving for the jewelry store to purchase Diana's gift, I recall. "Can I borrow your wagon?"

"Sure. It's parked out back of my house," Judith replies. "Don't worry about Sam, we'll take good care of her. Go see about your wife."

I leave the wagon parked on the curb next to a park and walk the last half block to the hospital. I'm not sure which door to enter, so I go inside the Emergency entrance and get in line to talk to the young woman inside a glass cage. My turn comes in another ten minutes— which seems like ten hours I am so anxious for news about Diana.

"My name is David Goldman. My wife Diana came here over an hour ago—she's in labor. Where is she? I need to see her."

"Calm down, young man, the waiting room for maternity patients is on the third floor. Take the stairs up at the end of the hall and tell the person at the desk you are looking for your wife," I am told.

"Thank you."

I hurry down the hallway and run up the stairs to the third floor. Four other men are pacing the waiting room as I approach the elderly man at the desk. "I'm looking for Diana Goldman."

He checks a list. "No one by that name is listed."

"That's impossible!" Fear shoots through me. "She has to be here because she's pregnant. My neighbor said she went into labor."

"Who's her doctor?" the man inquires.

I bite my lip. "I don't know if she was seeing anyone special. We usually went to the free clinic on 10th street for her checkups."

"Go back downstairs and ask the woman behind the glass cage to find out where your wife was taken," he orders. "Sorry I can't help."

Me, too! I am aggravated. This is Christmas Eve! Tonight is a holy night for Christians, and not supposed to be filled with fear.

What about no sickness, or tears, or pain, as recorded in the Old Testament during the time Jesus reigns? Is it because Diana and I are Gentiles? Is God's mercy only for Jews? I believed life would be perfect when Jesus returned to earth. Seems I was wrong.

Then, maybe God has reserved a more perfect time in the future when a new world exists. These things are beyond my understanding.

# 26

## Christmas Day

**I HAD SPENT ALL** night at Mercy Hospital in the waiting room with no news about Diana or our unborn child. My nerves were shredded as I prayed for strength to get through Christmas Day. With my head hanging wearily, I feel a hand on my shoulder and look up. The person is wearing a white toga, so I perceive he is an angel on a mission.

"Yes?" I grapple to my feet.

"Are you David Goldman?"

"Yes. Do you have news about my wife, Diana?"

"Come with me."

He leads me up a flight of stairs to the 2$^{nd}$ floor and into a compact office. "Wait here. The doctor will see you soon."

Soon turns into an eternity. Something is not right. I know Diana is in this hospital, yet no one has told me where, or allowed me to see her. I can only think the worst has happened. She's miscarried.

I stand up as a tall, lean man wearing a white apron over his clothes enters the office. "Sorry to keep you waiting, Mr. Goldman."

"Is my wife and child, okay?"

He shakes his head. "Baby's fine. Your wife passed."

*Passed to where?* "She was taken elsewhere?"

"No, son . . ." his strong hand grips my shoulder, "she died."

*Died?* No, no, no, no . . . this cannot be happening. Tears sting my eyes as I internalize a pain I have never experienced.

*Death has no sting?* It does for me. I drop to my knees.

"Here . . ." he pours me a glass of water as I stand.

"I know this is a shock—especially on Christmas Day, but there is some good news." He pauses while I thirstily drink the water.

"What can be good about this news?" I dash the glass against the counter and it shatters—just like my life—just like my world.

"Your son is a healthy 5 and ½ pound boy," the doctor reports. "He will need to stay at the hospital until he's gained some weight. In light of what's happened, there will be no charge for his care."

*No charge?* I think about that.

"What did you do to Diana?  Did someone make a mistake and kill her?"  I am all over bad scenarios about malpractice.

"Do you want to see your son?"

"Yes, and I need to see a written report—in detail—everything that was done to Diana from the time she came to this hospital."

"Of course," he says rather stiffly.

The nursery is on the 4th floor. My son's too fragile for me to hold until he's released from the hospital. Diana intended to name our daughter Grace. If we had a boy, Joseph after my father.

"You're shaking, son.  Do you want someone to drive you home?" the doctor asks.  "You can't see Diana's body until tomorrow."

"Why not?" I'm trembling. I'm sick to my stomach and angry, all at once. Christmas will never be joyful again for me.

"She's been taken to the morgue for burial preparation."

"I want her cremated."

"We don't do that in Israel.  Our bodies will be transformed at the end of the Millennium into an eternal state," he informs me.

I am too weak to argue.

"Shall I call a taxi?"

I nod in agreement. I will fetch Judith's wagon tomorrow morning.  Tonight, I need to hold Samantha in my arms. Too tired by the time the taxi let me out at Greta's house, I enter the dark abode and discover I am alone. Greta must be over at Judith's house.

I cannot think about what I'll face tomorrow.  I'm too sad.

There's a cold mist stirring in the atmosphere outdoors, but inside the house is warm and cozy.  Someone set a fire in the hearth. I sit in front of the Christmas tree and regard my life slipping off the deep end of grief.  Nothing I planned before leaving for Jerusalem has happened.

Life is unpredictable—joy and sadness intermingled.

For some reason, in my mind's eyes, I see the room in the Temple where the chosen priests offer blood sacrifices for the people.  A hot fire consumes the unblemished animals, demonstrating God's power to extinguish sin. This act is symbolic of what Jesus did on the cross when His body was torn and sacrificed for the sins of humankind.

The animal blood is washed away in a basin by water flowing from a deep spring rising up in the floor. The altar is cleansed. The sins of the Israel nation are wiped away—as if they did not exist. The sacrificial custom began millennia ago. During the Church Age, Christians were baptized, immersed in water, to signify cleansing.

Even the natural spring flowing beneath the Millennial Temple toward the south strengthens as it flows south to Egypt. It's force gathers and enlarges, like God's calling for repentance across the world. Jesus still offers mercy to each new generation birthed.

*The Living Water cleanses the land and produces healing trees.*

I sat quietly a moment, just thinking about salvation.

*Why, King Jesus? Why take Diana?*

A still small voice invades my consciousness.

*Life, son. Life.*

# 27

SMALL HANDS TOUCH MY face.  I open my eyes and realize I have slept on the floor in front of the Christmas tree for hours.  Samantha sits beside me, rubbing my face gently.  Curious about me.

I glance up and see that Greta has returned home. She offers me a hand and I rise to my feet, Sam tugging at my leg to pick her up.  The sunlight streams brightly through the window and dances on the floor.

I am too weary and too sad over Diana's death to speak.

Greta seems to sense my mood and hugs me.  Sam clings to one leg as I try to remain standing.  It's been a long twenty-four hours and I have not eaten since noon yesterday.  Have I even had water?

"I'm sorry about Diana," Greta says.

I only nod as I pick up my daughter and caress her.

"Mama?" she peeps.

"She's with Jesus," I say, a tear sliding down my face.

Sam squeezes my nose, seemingly content with my answer. When King Jesus held her in His arms while we were visiting with Him, I wonder if Sam felt a connection.  If He has Mama, Mama is good.

But I also know the human body stays in the grave until the end of the thousand-year reign of Christ, when He will raise the dead and judge sinners. Souls not cleansed by the blood of Jesus will be sentenced to live in darkness with Satan and his minions for eternity.

I have no concept of eternity, but know it is a very long time.

Then Earth will be cleansed by fire and recreated.  Every saved soul will receive a new body and a white stone signifying—I'm not sure.  No one has written an explanation that satisfies the question.

All of this future is out of my control.  I have one goal in front of me: to take care of Samantha as if she is my own child, and get my newborn boy out of the hospital.  We will return to my village in Brazil.

"Have you eaten anything this morning?" Greta asks.

"No.  I should, and drink some water."  My mouth is parched.

"I'll make us breakfast."

I snag Greta on the arm.  "Thank you."

"For what?" Her marble black German eyes sparkle.

"Taking care of Diana when I wasn't here."

She nods, tears in her gaze. "I'll get us some food."

Sam trots after Greta, having grown fond of the elderly widow since we moved into her upstairs apartment eight weeks ago. I am weary, but realize I'll need strength to face whatever comes my future.

I have to bury Diana. I have to make plans to go home. So, I'll need to hire a nanny to travel with me. The trip will be difficult.

What will Dahlia say when she sees my two children?

# 174 ACR

## 28

**THE TRIP HOME HAS** been arranged. It is March. I've paid Benjamin in full for our passages on his fine boat. He's jolly as usual as I step aboard with little Joseph in my arms. Three months old, he's a healthy baby named after my father. Greta steps aboard behind me, holding Sam's hand so she won't slip into the rippling water stirring the ship.

I think of Diana. Then put her out of my mind. I must concentrate on my family's future. Diana would not want me to grieve. If she taught me anything it is that life is difficult, unpredictable, but worthy of fighting for. She did just that—though she bled out while giving birth.

We will spend a few days in Port Guinea Bissau when we arrive in approximately six weeks. Ben does not get in any hurry. But I feel safe with him at the helm. He is good at being a ship captain and loves King Jesus as much as I do. That's a winning ticket to Bethel.

* * *

### Back in Bethel, Brazil

Joseph reread the letter David sent him weeks ago. His son had obtained passage on a ship headed to Port Guinea Bissau when he penned the message: *Father, I am on my way home. I pray you are doing well. Much has changed in my life.* Joseph had not told Dahlia about the letter.

Life had changed for her, too. She'd fallen in love with someone else, engaged and about to be married to Milo Sullivan, David's best friend. The wedding ceremony was scheduled for 2 p.m. today.

It did not seem wise to destroy the couple's plans by telling them about David's return. Thus, it seemed prudent to keep silent.

Joseph would attend the wedding, wish the newlyweds well, and try to put all negative thoughts out of his mind as he dressed to leave for Jupiter. There was much to celebrate with David's return.

* * *

Weeks have passed since he'd written to his father. David feels optimistic about returning to Bethel with his family—though absent a mother. He intends to raise his son and daughter to be responsible Christians.  He knows Dahlia will be a wonderful mother to his children. She is the embodiment of beauty and all that is good life.

Hopefully, his father received his letter he'd sent, and told Dahlia he was coming home. He expects they will throw a party for him.

The breeze on the Mediterranean is swift today—April showers blowing constantly in the wind. Greta is on deck watching Benjamin navigate the ship south in the Atlantic waters.  They'd spent their first night at sea on the ship then docked in Crete for two nights while Ben purchased more supplies for their trip to Port Guinea-Bissau in West Africa. Captain Ben doesn't get in any hurry; safety, his motto.

By the time we arrive at the port, it will be late in May.

I hold little Joseph in my arms, considering how much he will miss his mother as he grows older.  But Sam misses Diana now. He has yet to have a talk with her about death and grief. She won't understand.

"Sam?" I whisper in her ear. "Are you happy?"

The fifteen-month-old little girl is mentally superior to others her age.  She memorizes storybooks and understands what I say.

"Yes, Papa."  She laughs.  "Happy, happy, happy!"

I suppose all little girls are. Sam has bright almond-eyes the color of coal, and her small shape is perfect like Diana's.  I am thankful she will never suffer the sexual abuse her mother had in serving as a temple prostitute to Baal. Thor must never suspect that he has a daughter. He would travel across the world to claim her. Diana's daughter would be raised a heathen with ungodly principles. That must not happen.

"You have a grandfather that wants to see you," I tell Sam.

Her mystical eyes roll in thought.

"He's like me, a papa, but older," I explain.

"Grand Papa?"

Sam is so smart.  I wish I had a picture of Joseph to show her. I look a lot like him and he looks like our great-grandfather, Cory Lindsey. As Sam matures, I will teach her about our family history— the importance of treasuring the past so we can plan a better future.

Which makes me wonder what our world will look like in two, five, or even a thousand years. Will people recreate all the modern conveniences the world once enjoyed before Satan ruled the planet?

"Papa, are you sad?" Sam asks.

"No, sweetie." I pinch her nose. "Just thinking."

She giggles and puts her small hands over her lips.

"What's so funny, Sam?"

"Mama says the same thing sometimes."

"Mama is happier than you or me."

*Is she? Buried in a public cemetery south of Tel-Aviv?*

An autopsy had been performed to determine the cause of Diana's death. She bled out while giving birth to Joseph. I stood over her grave, praying she would sleep peacefully until Jesus raised her.

*Was she truly saved?*

This thought troubles me.

*Am I her judge?*

I've lied to Sam. I am not truly happy. I feel abandoned by God.

*Where is my faith to face the future?*

Yet, I am fortunate that Greta agreed to accompany us to Bethel. She'd sold her property and changed her *agoras* to gold coins—in case we needed extra funds. Our trip had been prepaid.

*Only God knows our future. God, help me cope better.*

# 29

**EVERYTHING THAT COULD GO** wrong had during our trip to Port Guinea-Bissau. Benjamin's ship survived four spring storms as we sailed south in the Atlantic Ocean. Supplies had to be tossed overboard to lighten the load—reminiscent of the story in the New Testament where Paul of Tarsus warned the captain and crew not to abandon the ship during a terrible storm. Like them, our sails were lowered as we gave the wind control and constantly drifted off course.

Instead of reaching our destined port in late May as planned, Captain Ben did not set the anchors in Jamestown until early July. Everyone aboard, including sailors, were skinny and travel-weary by that time. All the sailors talked about were finding girls for the night and getting drunk when we finally arrived. Greta seemed to handle our struggle to remain hopeful the best. At least, she never complained.

Greta had lived longer and learned that not giving up was the way to survival. I took note of her bravery, though I'd failed miserably.

But we did reach the port safely, thanks to our captain's wise decisions, and tested our land legs. It felt wonderful to touch solid ground. I wanted to fall on my face and kiss the green grass growing alongside the roadways. But I knew better than to worship nature.

Purple and yellow flowers blossom in front of huts and shelters since it's summertime, the warmest season of the year. I don't want to winter here again. Ben promised we'd only stay a week before setting sail for Jamestown. With no way of sending word that I was delayed aboard a ship and drifting; my father must believe I'm dead by now.

Passengers will stay at the Bissau Inn again. Antonia and Bonnie were beside themselves making over Samantha and little Joseph. She offered us a suite for the price of one room—her wedding gift. Where was Diana? I could not answer her, so Greta explained the situation.

 Bonnie prepared a pig in a backyard firepit for supper that night, and served the meat with new potatoes and carrots. She baked two apple pies—making sure her guests did not go hungry. And we didn't.

Greta, Sam, and I ate like it was our last meal. And, actually, no one really knows when that day is coming. Just be prepared.

We told stories after supper until late in the night. The children fell asleep in our laps, so we decided to call it a day. In fact, it had been a very long day. But a good one, considering the sad memories I'd left behind in Israel. My thoughts were already on home, and Dahlia.

* * *

## *Bethel, Brazil*

Milo had built a new cabin for his bride Dahlia. They had moved into the residence only two weeks before. Joseph knocked on their front door, his handcrafted gift in hand, a wooden cradle for the baby on the way. Only three months pregnant, it was early to give Dahlia such a gift, but it was intended to soften Joseph's news that he'd received a letter from David in March saying he was coming home.

The day the letter arrived was the day before Milo and Dahlia wed. Now that months had gone by, Milo needed to be warned of the possibility that David might soon return—if he survived his long journey. While Dahlia was in the kitchen making lemonade, Joseph removed the letter from his pants pocket and handed it to Milo.

"What's this?" Milo turns the letter over in his hand.

"Just read it, my friend."

While Milo reads and rereads the letter, Joseph waits.

"David's coming home?"

"Yes—was due here months ago," Joseph says. "Obviously, he's been delayed due to the long trip from Israel. But I thought you should know. He could show up any day now—if he's still alive."

"You're not sure."

Joseph shakes his head. "I only pray he's safe. I don't know what he meant in saying a lot has changed. Much has changed here, too."

"It sure has." Milo restlessly paces the small living room.

"Is something wrong?" Dahlia asks, carrying a tray with glasses of lemonade and sugar cookies as she returns to the living room.

Her eyes are on Milo, questioning. No doubt in Joseph's mind, they're in love. She's plump from pregnancy and more beautiful than ever. Joseph knows that David will be crushed when he learns that Dahlia has married his best friend. But it was Milo who was there for Dahlia after David left. He traveled to Jupiter twice a week to encourage her. It was inevitable that the two young people would gravitate to one another for comfort and eventually fall in love.

Joseph could not fault them for that. Hadn't he fallen in love with his deceased wife the first time they met? A marriage made in Heaven.

"Let's go out the front porch and have our refreshments," Milo suggests to Joseph. "Best you stay inside, Dahlia."

She nods. "Whatever you say, Milo." She knows he will tell her everything said when they are alone. They have no secrets.

The conversation is not pleasant. Facts are facts and cannot be altered by emotional responses. What's done is done. Over.

Joseph does not tarry long before returning to his cabin. Since David's departure, he's totally remodeled their living quarters. His son will have much to report concerning his visit to Israel and private time spent with King Jesus. His success has reached Bethel. It's been raining regularly for weeks. The village knew David succeeded.

* * *

It is bedtime when Milo decides to show Dahlia the letter David sent his father. Like him, she reads it over several times.

"He never wrote to me."

"I know, honey. If he had, we—uh . . ."

"Would not have married and I would not be carrying your child." Dahlia's eyes are heavy with sleep. "We can't go back now, Milo."

He nods. "The dye is cast."

Dahlia smiles. "David will understand."

"Will he?" Milo has been conflicted since Joseph's visit.

"Don't torture yourself, love."

"I can't help it. I am—or was—David's best friend. Who treats a friend badly and steals his bride-to-be while he's on a mission trip? He will hate us both when he learns we have not waited for him."

"Perhaps you misjudge David. He's a good person. And the letter did say his circumstances have changed. Let's wait and see what happens when he returns before we get all bent out of shape."

Milo hugs Dahlia. "I got mighty lucky woman when I married you. The wise one of this family, but don't forget I wear the pants."

Dahlia laughs. "I can't fit into your pants, anyhow."

They both laugh.

# 30

**IT RAINED THE NEXT FOUR** days in Port Guinea-Bissau. I was surprised when the nun Beverly from Australia checked into the inn. She had not heard about Diana's death, so I had to revisit that conversation painfully. Would my grief never end? Maybe when I set eyes on Dahlia, I would receive comfort. I hope she waited for me.

As promised, we set sail for Jamestown a week later. The ship had been repaired and Ben has added new sails. We'd packed our bags, paid our bill for a week's stay at Bissau Inn, and departed.

Ben has room for Beverly to travel with us. She is delighted to help Greta with the children, giving me free time to pray and read my Bible. The more I think about home, the more I dread showing up in Bethel with my new family. What will the villagers think of me?

He leaves at age sixteen and returns nearly three years later with two children and a nanny? I'm tormented by where life has taken me.

But Diana would have died at Thor's hands if I had left her behind in Jamestown. Benjamin had talked me into marrying her since she was already pregnant. All of that had been out of my control. I'd done the best I could to be an honorable husband. But Joseph was a surprise.

If only I had taken off work on Christmas Eve and stayed home with Diana! I would have been there to take her to the hospital. Maybe, life would have turned out differently—if something had been changed. But I cannot go back and relive those moments. They are gone. All that is left is the future. And my choices. Good and bad.

* * *

We pulled into the port of Jamestown in late September. This trip across the Atlantic Ocean went smoothly. Greta and Beverly became good friends. We had only been there a week when Greta decided she would return to Australia with Beverly—which did not make me happy since I was losing a nanny. How am I to travel home with two children?

Benjamin finds me drinking ale at a pub to wash away my worries. Somehow, today my faith fails me even more. Life is out of control.

"Tis not like ya son to drink alcohol." He sits on the stool by me.

"I know, but I found out today that Greta will not be returning with me to Bethel. I need to hire a nanny. Know of someone?"

"Drinkin' Ale won't solv' that pro'lem, David."

"I know. But alcohol calms my nerves."

"Look, I know of a widow recently lost her hus'ben. I'll go witch ya to see her tomorrow—to give you a good refer'nce, if ya want."

David sets the ale aside. "I'm scared, Ben."

He laughs. "You? A strong Christian who saw Jesus?"

David rolls the stool toward Ben. "Of going home. What it everything in Bethel is different? And there's Dahlia."

*What will she think of me?*

"Ya caint hep what's done, son. Ya' father misses ya."

"I know he does. Still . . ."

"Hire a nanny and go home, David. See fer yoursef."

The next day I take Ben's suggestion. He goes with me to talk to Widow Young. She's in her mid-twenties and has no children.

After hearing of my tragedy in losing Diana and Greta's decision to no longer help me with my children, she agrees to accompany me to Bethel. Now I am bringing home a pretty young woman and two children with me. What will the villagers think of me when I arrive?

*What will Dahlia say?*

* * *

I found a boat headed west by river and paid for four passengers. Hank the Captain looked like a pirate, spit tobacco when he wasn't smoking a pipe, and had a foul mouth that spewed curse words.

Widow Young was terrified, and kept my children as far from him as she could. She talked little and followed directions. Little Joseph took to her quickly. I soon learned the widow had been married for ten years and could not bear children. This was a winning situation.

Before we were three hours out of Jamestown, our fishing vessel was attacked. Hank used a shotgun to kill three of the six thugs attempting to steal the boat and its cargo. They would kill us all if they succeeded, so I used a knife to protect Widow Young and my children.

When the skirmish ended, Hank made his young captive tell us where he came from—how he knew we were sailing west. We learned the young lad was from Rebellion and his band of cutthroats were sent to look for and bring back a girl named Samantha. No longer able to keep silent, I intervened with questions. "What do you mean?"

"I only follow orders," he nervously answered.

"How do you know my daughter?"

The young thug's eyes skitter from mine to Hank's.

"Tell 'im, boy, or I'll cut out your tongue!"

"Thor says the girl is his daughter," the boy replies.

"Wan' me to kill this kidnapper and thief?" Hank asks me.

I inhale, thrusting murder out of my thoughts.

"I don't wan' no trouble. Jus' doin' my job," he says.

"Do you have proof that Samantha is Thor's daughter?" I inquire.

"Is this true?" Hank curses. "She's not your daughter?"

"May I explain before you judge me?" I plead with Hank.

The thief named Grey is pushed ashore by Hank to discuss the situation. I explain to Hank how Diana followed me out of Rebellion and would have been killed if she returned, so I married her before departing for Israel on Benjamin Cohn's ship. Grey listens, but will not speak since Hank's knife is handily at his throat. One look at Hank and no one wants to fight him. Certainly not Grey.

"Tomorrow, I want you off my boat," Hank tells me.

"How will I get home?" My heart sinks as fear takes hold. "I have a family, and a young widow traveling with me."

"Not my problem," Hank says. "You can go." He cuts the ropes to Grey's wrists. "Get outta here now!"

The young thief runs, disappearing into the forest thickets lining the riverside. "He'll tell Thor how to find us," I tell Hank.

"Not my problem."

"Please. You're sentencing my family to death."

"As I said, not my problem. You have till sunrise."

# 31

## *The Wilderness*

**WHAT ARE YOU DOING?** Widow Young asks David. He's on his knees with his head bowed, muttering something she cannot understand. He is unresponsive and that troubles her.

"David! Get up!" she demands. "I can't manage your children alone. We have to do something. We cannot just stand here idly."

He does not move, except for his lips.

Amelia nudges him on the arm. Little Joseph and Samantha are crying and she cannot console them. "David! Get up, I need your help!" It's a last-ditch effort to move him while standing in the wilderness. They are stranded by a fast-flowing river, nothing but forests and mountains surrounding them. It's a hopeless situation.

*Dear Jesus, you see our need for help,* David silently prays, aware that the Widow Young stands over him, harassing him. *I bless Your name. I am yours, Lord. Show me how to save my family. Help us, please!*

"David!" Amelia sits on the ground next to him. "What can I do to help? Your children are distressed and weary. Do something."

*I hear your prayer, David. Trust me. Walk south and I will show you what to do next. Get up. Your family needs you.*

David opens his eyes and rises to his feet. "Let's go."

Amelia looks up at him. She is petite, a mere five-foot two inches tall and weighs less than one-hundred twenty pounds. She is not a pretty girl, but her golden hair is natural, and her hazel eyes reflect a glimmer of intelligence. Her grandfather was an engineer, was trained as a youngster by his father concerning the specific construction of things. He could make anything, she recalls. He was skilled.

"Where?" Amelia finds her voice as she gathers the children to her; Joseph in her arms, Sam by a hand. They have stopped crying.

David points to a mountain lying to the south. "Up there."

"No, we should follow the riverbed west," Amelia advises. "It will take us to a village eventually. The mountain is too treacherous."

David looks down at the widow. "You use big words."

"I was educated.  I can think for myself."

"Then, think this: God told me to go south," David explains.  "I trust we'll encounter something or someone that can help us."

Amelia nods. Not a Christian, she trusts David's connection with Jesus.  And he's her boss.  She grins.

"You think this is funny?" David gathers Joseph into his arms. "Us, out in the wilderness alone.  With two little ones?"

Amelia shakes her head. "No, boss, I only follow."

So, David leads . . .

Two hours later, they are deep in the wooded terrain.  David uses a hatchet to cut away the branches as they walk.

"How much farther?" Amelia asks. "My shoes are getting holes."

"I don't know."  David jerks a breath.  "We keep walking."

And they did.  Over the next ridge, they spy a nice compact cabin—it looks brand-new.  No choice, but to explore.

"What if the occupant is dangerous?"

"What if he's not?" David counters.  "Let's see."

And they do.

David pushes open the door and glances around. "Hello!"

No response.

He motions for Amelia to come inside with the children.

"Anybody home?" he calls out loudly.

No response.

"See if there is food and water in the kitchen," he instructs Amelia. "I'll take a look around to see if we're safe."

There are two bedrooms.  Both furnished with beds, dressers, and clothes in the closets. *Where is the owner?*

There is an indoor privy off the hallway that leads to a covered back porch.  The cabin stands in a grassy plain on a ledge overlooking a valley below.  The owner cannot be far away.  It's a wilderness.

David returns to the vaulted great room featuring a fireplace with chunks of aged wood lying on the hearth to build a fire.  It is October, not cold enough to need warmth, but this owner is prepared.

Amelia returns to the great room carrying two mugs of hot tea. "I found the kitchen stocked," she tells David.  "Where is the owner?"

"I don't know.  But this must be a gift from Jesus."  He stares down at Amelia.  "We will spend the night here; see if anyone comes."

"And if they don't?" Amelia hands David his mug of tea.

"We will winter here and make a plan in the spring."

The tea is a rich brew with added honey. David wonders if an angel prepared this cabin for them. The Jews are blessed by their Messiah. The prophecies of the Old Testament are being fulfilled. Saints born before the Great Flood that destroyed humankind dwell in Jerusalem with the martyrs who died for their faith in Jesus during the Tribulation. The Twelve Apostles of Jesus commune with Old Testament priests and prophets.

This era in history, this reign of Christ, is like no other time in history. The lion and the lamb lie down beside each other. Wars between nations have ceased. Peace surpasses all understanding.

Night falls and David locks the cabin doors—not that he expects any visitors in the wilderness. It just feels safer to be inside the cabin with his two children.  And Amelia, of course.  God has placed her in his life.  He needs to consider marrying her. Living with him will appear sinful to others.  He'll need her help when they arrive in Bethel.

*What will Dahlia think of his arrangement?*

# 32

**NO ONE RETURNS TO** the cabin. Ever. David and Amelia spend the winter on the mountainside. He hunts for deer, which they freeze-dry and convert to jerky. Amelia is a good cook, and the kitchen pantry is well-stocked. It's a mystery who built this cabin and stocked it. For them, it appears. David realizes someone was told to build this cabin and stock it for the winter. Maybe, they never intended to live here.

It's comforting to realize how well-prepared God is in planning our futures—especially His sheep that follow Him without question. David has made mistakes in his life. Sinned in thought, on occasions. But he has never doubted Jesus is Lord! He'd knelt to worship Him.

By April, Little Joseph is fifteen months old and Sam turned two this past January. Amelia is quiet and obedient, talking little about her feelings or her troubled past. David is fond of her, but not in love. His heart belongs to Dahlia. But he'd shared it once with Diana.

One bright spring morning, Amelia asks, "When are we leaving?"

I glance up, sighing. "Soon, I hope."

She sits on the sofa, conflicted.

"Do you know the way to your village?"

"No, I don't." And that puts a frown on her face.

"We cannot strike out in the wilderness without a plan, David. It's too hard a journey for the children to travel on foot. And they are too heavy for us to carry," Amelia points out. "Be sensible."

"I will," I assure her. "We'll wait here until God tells me what to do." This is not like her to question me. "I trust Jesus to help us."

"Why?" she asks. "How can you be so sure He's listening?"

"I know it in my heart. He's Creator and Lord of the Universe."

"Maybe he's a false messiah," Amelia argues.

"No. Jesus is the only Messiah! God's only Son," I counter.

"How can you be so sure?"

"Jesus' birth was foretold by the Old Testament prophets. He came as a baby, born to a Virgin named Mary, grew up in Nazareth, and became a carpenter like his adopted father, Joseph."

"Then who is Jesus' real father?"

"God," I tell her. "If we have faith in Jesus that His death on a Roman cross cancels out sin, we will be eternally saved."

"I'm only interested in saving us, David."

"Read the Bible," I insist. "Then I'll answer your questions."

A tear trickles down Amelia's cheek.

"I'll pray for you."

Her upper lip trembles. "May I borrow your Bible?"

"Of course. 'Seek and you will find', the scriptures tell us."

I get God's Word from my bedroom and hand it to Amelia. She holds it in her hands like it's fragile. "Be careful, it's old, "I warn.

She nods. "I will. You have a lot of faith in Jesus."

"Yes, I do. Maybe we are still here because of you."

Amelia startles. "What do you mean, David?"

"Perhaps God has detained us until you come to him. Read God's Word written by Jesus' apostles and I promise your life will be changed for the good." I stare at Amelia, apparently bewildered.

She carries my Bible to her bedroom and closes the door as I gather Sam in my lap. "Wanna take your brother for a long walk?"

A few minutes later, we are making out way down a trodden path leading to the opposite side of the mountain from where the cabin stands. It's a rugged pathway, but I need to give Amelia time alone without interference from my children. I see someone coming.

"Hello there!" I warily call out, praying we are safe.

"Good tidings to you, David!" the stranger hails back.

"How do you know my name?" We stand face to face.

"Jesus told me a couple of weeks back that you needed my help," remarks the elderly fellow with thick, curly gray hair and a bushy beard. "Perhaps you're in need of a guide?  Hmm . . . am I right?"

"Do you know the way to Bethel?" I gather Sam closer.

"Aye."

"A nanny travels with us.  What's your name?"

"Folks call me Dutch."

"Dutch."  David shakes the man's hand.

"I'll help you get packed for the journey," he offers.

"I don't need your help, thank you."

"No, thank Jesus.  Helping you is His idea, not mine."

* * *

When we get to the cabin, it feels empty.

"Where can she be?" I ask Dutch.  He only shakes his head. "I told Amelia to wait here while I took the children for a walk."

"Hmm . . is she prone to disobedience?" he asks.

"What kind of question is that?"

"The obvious," he replies.

Dutch appears to be a hunter since he's dressed in camouflage clothing and carries a shotgun holstered over one shoulder. He's a burly man the size of a gorilla, and just as hairy. A little scary.

"Where do you think Amelia has gone?" he inquires.

"I don't know. She took my Bible to her bedroom to read.  I wanted to give her time to think about accepting Jesus as her Savior."

"Aye, makes sense," Dutch comments. "Perhaps she's rejected God's Word and has left your company.  Did you coerce her?"

I can't help from glaring. "No. Amelia is a good person!"

"It's wrong to pressure people to accept Christ."

"Who are you, my preacher?" I react, upsetting Joseph. The infant sniffles, then boo-hoos.  I am beside myself with what to do.

"We'll find Nan-Na, Joe. Hush little boy. How 'bout a snack? Apple juice sound good?" I do my best to comfort him.

Dutch stands like a statue, waiting for me to make a decision. I can tell his patience is wearing out. "You should pack up and let's go now.  Time is important.  We can't afford to waste it on your nanny."

*Is something bad about to happen?* I question.

"I'm only here to help you, friend, not Amelia."

"Isn't that a little cold?  I won't leave this cabin without her. Amelia wouldn't last an hour fending for herself in the wilderness!"

My thoughts tumble with indecision. I am responsible more for the safety of my children than a nanny I hired. But I won't leave her.

"Fine.  You go out and look for her," Dutch says. "I'll wait here." He picks up Joseph and sits on the sofa, bouncing him on his lap.

All of this seems so weird. *Jesus, show me what to do.*

"Go get the juice and we'll be fine.  Won't we, son?"

Sam dances over with a storybook in one hand.  "Read to me?" She plops down on the sofa beside Dutch, tickling Joseph's feet.

First, I search the house to see if Amelia has left me a note—at least she owes me that. I find no clue to where she's gone, so I go outside through the backdoor and walk around the cabin.

*Is it possible Thor found us and took her?*

After searching for over an hour in the woods surrounding the cabin, I give up and return to the cabin. By then, it is approaching dusk.

As I enter through the front door, the odor of food slaps me in the face. I hear noises coming from the kitchen. I discover Dutch and the children seated at the breakfast table, and Amelia at the counter.

She looks happy, joyful, and that makes me angry.

"Where have you been, Amelia? I've looked everywhere for you."

"I decided to take a walk," she explains while icing cookies.

"I specifically told you to stay here. Why didn't you listen?"

She arches her back and faces me. "No, you told me to read the Bible and think about accepting Jesus as my Savior."

"That, too. Did you?"

"Yes, and I confessed my sins and asked the Holy Spirit to come into my life and guide me," Amelia reports. "I felt so good I decided to take a walk in the woods to pray. I fell asleep against a tree."

"I didn't see you, and I've been looking for hours." I can't help being irritated at wasting time. "I'm pleased you are a Christian, but I need to trust you, Amelia. You could have at least left me a note."

"I'm sorry, David. I just didn't think about it."

"Are we all good now?" Dutch intervenes. "We'll spend the night here and leave for your village at first light. Let's eat and go to bed."

*Are we?* Amelia touches David's hand.

I jerk away. The last thing I want in my life is a woman who will abandon me and my children. First, Diana. Then, Greta.

"I'll feed the children and put them to bed early," she offers.

"Good!" Dutch exclaims. "After supper, David and I need to go over my plan. Won't be easy taking ya'll through the woods." He pauses to look up as if seeing someone. "But, I will, if God allows."

# 33

**WE LEFT THE CABIN** at First Light. The weather is spring-like as Dutch carries Sam while I hold Joseph close to my heart. The widow feels poorly—a spider bite, she thinks. We travel slowly on foot.

I have no idea where Dutch is leading us. Finally, I ask.

"Uh, do you have a plan in mind, Dutch?"

He stops in the middle of a valley and surveys the mountains surrounding us. "Trusting Jesus to direct me."

*What?* I think about the uncertainty of his plan.

He looks down, studies me like I'm an infidel. "You don't trust Jesus to guide us? Isn't that lack of faith? Man up, David!"

"I have to think about my family, and the widow. I can't just trust Fate. Or you. I need to know where we are going. Right now!"

Dutch bows his head while the four of us wait for a decision. I want to turn around and go back to the cabin. We were safe there. But, didn't the Israelites trailing Moses feel the same way? They had rather be in bondage to the Egyptians than to face a desert wilderness. This was no different. They lacked faith. So do I. Dutch opens his eyes.

"Over that ridge." He points. "We go there and decide."

"Okay," I agree. Then notice Amelia has slumped against a tree trunk. I walk over and feel her head. She's burning with fever.

"She's sick?" Dutch nods. "Can she still walk?"

"Amelia!" I shake her. "She won't wake up."

Dutch plants his big hand on his wide hips. *Humph.*

"No, we cannot just leave her here!" I declare.

"We'll camp here until she wakes up," Dutch decides.

"How long?" It is still morning. We are only a few hours from the cabin. Maybe we should go back and delay the trip till she's better."

I don't want to do that, but what choice do we have?

"No, I have medicine for fever. I'll give it to the widow and we will wait right here," Dutch says, and I will not argue. He's in charge.

* * *

Amelia remains sleeping as darkness cloaks us in the open valley. Her left ankle is swollen and blue. Dutch grabs a tent from his backpack and sets it up. "She'll sleep inside with the children," he tells me. "There's a south breeze blowing. We'll camp here by a fire."

I know how to build a fire; my father taught me. I gather sticks from the nearby clump of trees and use a flint to ignite the larger limbs mixed in with small chips of wood I have shaved off with my knife. I cannot help but recall my father's warning the morning I left my village for Israel: Be prepared, son. There are many dangers ahead of you.

June 16, I'll be away from home for three years. I cannot imagine what Dahlia is doing right now. She's nineteen, a full-grown woman, and should be married. Is she willing to be chastised as an Old Maid?

Dutch and I sit silently as flames flash and twist like demons leaping inside the firepit. I think of Hades and am grateful I am a Christian. Satan and the False Prophet are locked away. All they have to look forward to is a final judgment when the Millennium ends.

That's a long way off. Or so it seems to me. I won't live to see it, but hopefully my offspring will. But the future is sketchy.

"Tell me about yourself, David." Dutch breaks the silence.

"What do you want to know?"

"What made you decide to travel to Jerusalem to praise King Jesus? Are you even twenty yet?"

"Turn nineteen in June." I think of Rebellion, and Thor, and Diana, and what a drama all that was for years in my life. I married her, a prostitute, so she could escape her fate in Baal worship. I had no idea she was pregnant with Thor's baby when we wed on Benjamin's ship.

"Your silence tells me nothing," Dutch interrupts my thoughts.

"My father Joseph taught me the Scriptures from the time I could walk. My mother died when I was young. It had not rained in our village for decades. Nobody made and effort to leave their homes and worship Jesus in Jerusalem. I thought I should be the one."

Dutch nods. "That's why you are so important to Jesus."

"How do you know that?"

"I am less than a man."

"You are an angel—in human form."

"Yes, so you need to relax and trust my judgment. I get my instructions directly from Jesus. Amelia will be better tomorrow; Jesus said so, and He's never wrong. Let's get some sleep."

# 34

**I SLEPT BETTER LAST** night, knowing Jesus has sent an angel to watch over my family and lead us home. Despite my reservations, Amelia is much better this morning. The spring day is sunny, a southerly breeze blowing. Only a few hours from the cabin where we'd wintered, I am anxious to see what is over the next ridge.

We soon break camp and start our journey again. Manna was for breakfast. Found it on a rocky surface. Imagine! I aways wondered what it tasted like—where it came from. It is sweet like honey, crisp, and filling. Samantha gathers a handful and merrily tosses them into the breeze. They sail high and drift like snowflakes.

"Eat it now. Won't last through the day," Dutch warns.

I am reminded how Moses instructed the Israelites to not store the manna for the next day. Some of God's blessings are meant for the moment. We will enjoy and be thankful. So, I eat my fair share.

Over the next ridge we face a surprise. There is a raging river cutting through the rocky terrain at the base. It is wide and looks too dangerous to cross on foot. Dutch slides down the mountain side and stands on the rocky banks. No choice but to follow.

The odor of fish suggests we catch some. Dutch thinks it's a fine idea. He even has a fishing pole and bait inside his bag. None like none I've seen before. The pole folds in sections upon itself. A handy little invention he picked up somewhere. Amelia caught the first fish.

Her laughter makes me think of Peter and John back in Bible Times. They were catching fish when Jesus came along and told Peter he would become a fisher of men. Over a firepit, we sear the fish in a frying pan, eat our fair share, then sit in the warm sunshine until noon.

I'm not in charge, but it feels like we're wasting time. What is Dutch waiting for? Like, how can we cross the river? Our problem is soon solved when a floating raft sails around the bend in swift waters.

Two stout men using long poles to guide their craft spy us and float over to the river's edge. The men leap off the raft then heft the craft upon the rocky beach. The older man disappears behind a bush to do his thing. The younger man stares, more interested in us.

While I thought we were wasting time, Dutch was waiting for King Jesus to solve our problem. I need to be more like our leader.

"What're ya doin' out here in the wild'ness?" the teen asks.

Though Dutch claims he's in charge, I feel the question is aimed at me. "We were waiting for somebody to rescue us," I explain.

The elderly man walks back and shakes my hand.

"Name's Sawyer, and this here is my nephew, Jason."

"Good timing, fellows," Dutch says. "These hard rocks are getting uncomfortable. Can you help us out?"

"Hop a'board, we got plen'y of room!" Jason offers.

"Thanks," I utter, but don't think either one heard me. They were busy discussing the best way to get us aboard and the weight equal.

Dutch helps Amelia onto the raft. While she is seated, he hands her Joseph. I get on next and take Sam in my arms. Dutch stands on the rocky beach, doesn't move. "This is where I get off."

"You're not coming the rest of the way with us?" I ask.

"Just got another assignment. Fellows here seems capable."

"Wher' you goin', son?" Sawyer looks at me.

"Bethel. My home village. These children are mine. Amelia is their nanny." *Not my wife.* It seems important I clarify that fact.

"I know wher' it is," Jason pipes. "Can take you close enough ya'can walk rest of the way." The two adventurers set the raft afloat.

I look back to wave at Dutch, but he's not there. I wonder if he went over the ridge where we'd come from, or simply disappeared.

I will never understand how all that angel stuff works.

# 35

IT'S WARM IN THE Southern Hemisphere. Before Christ returned, the month of May signaled the onset of winter. But the climate is changing. A hot breeze blows from the south through the valley as the bright sun sizzles in the mid-day sky. Dahlia's baby is due any day now.

She sits on the front porch of their eighteen-month-old cabin and watches the children play kickball in the street, hoping she will bear a son who will learn Milo's trade as an expert carpenter. He'd built their cabin by himself; cut the trees, planed the wood, sliced it in the right lengths, and put the structure together like one does Lego pieces.

No nails, it's a beautiful work of art. She rocks, but all is not perfect. David's father Joseph has not revisited them since last fall. Dahlia is confident he hasn't received further word from David.

It worries her that he is long overdue. Perhaps, he's encountered trouble. He might be dead. But if not, what will he think of her when he learns she's married his best friend and is pregnant?

*Will he hate them both? Forever? Never forgiving?*

The thought of David never coming home grieves her as the little one tosses restlessly inside her body, waiting to make an entrance into this world. Dahlia was her mother's fifth child, the second girl. Two of her siblings had died in infancy. It was a dangerous world to bring a baby into—but life goes on as it has done since the First Couple.

* * *

David cannot help thinking about Dahlia now that he is within a week of returning home. Sawyer and Jason have been fantastic. Jason especially has taken a liking to the widow. David can only hope Amelia will not abandon him for another life when he needs her service so dearly in caring for his young children. Diana had been a good mother, but she had not lived long enough to truly enjoy motherhood.

The raft drifts over to the side of the tributary as the stream grows smaller. Eventually the raging river had become only a trickle with little energy to pull it deeper into the countryside. They had drifted across the border into Brazil a week ago, three weeks since Dutch left them.

David helps Amelia off the boat first. Her gaze is on Jason.

*Troubling.*

"Will you come to Bethel to visit me?" she shyly asks Jason.

*They are falling in love.*

"Count on it, Angela." Jason's smile is silly, but joyful.

Without comment, Sawyer hands Joseph to the widow then places Sam on the rocky bank. "Go south. There's a trail—can't get lost."

I laugh. "You'd be surprised, Sawyer! I've been lost most of my adult life." I'm not speaking of spiritually, but rather how I've muddled through life since departing Bethel nearly three years ago.

"Life's what ya make it." He huffs. "Home 'll feel good."

"Yes, it will," I agree. "But I'm sure life there has changed."

"Life always changes, friend." Sawyer gives Jason a hand to board the raft. "We must be goin' now. Good luck to ya' all."

I stand on the bank and wave as the raft turns around to head back half a mile and take another tributary. Sawyer never said where they were headed, their final destination. It is none of my business.

But I cannot help wondering if Sawyer is an angel in disguise. He seemed so willing to help us. It was not a natural human trait. Jason was definitely human. His male hormones were working just fine.

So were Amelia's. She'll be married to someone by next spring.

* * *

Somehow, we got off the trail by mistake. We spent the first night nestled in a cave at the foot of a mountain. But, close enough to civilization hear the rushing water of Angel Falls farther south.

Little Joseph was fussy and tired of traveling. Amelia was good with Sam—kept her busy with coloring books and stories about mythical characters. I tried to be positive about going home.

I dreaded facing Dahlia. I had failed her miserably.

The fire faded out as night grew darker and it began to storm. I prayed that Bethel was getting its fair share of rain after all the trauma I'd been through in making my trip to Israel. Then I slept, too.

* * *

The next thing I know it is morning. Amelia is screaming to the top of her lungs, "Wake up, David! Samantha's gone!"

*Gone.* I sit up and shake out my stiff body. Sleeping on a rock is no way to get a good night's rest. "She's just scouting."

"Scouting." Amelia says the word like I've lost my mind.

"She's around." I crawl to my feet and shuffle down the cliff to the base. "Sam! Quit hiding from us! Where are you?"

But no voice breaks the forest sounds of birds tweeting and animals howling in the distance. "Sam!" I try again. "Samantha!"

We look everywhere and do not find my daughter.

Amelia drops to the ground. "They took her."

I sit down next to the widow. "Who took her?"

"Thor, and his bunch of thugs."

"No way!" I deny the thought. "If he's been trailing us, he would have taken her long ago. We are nine weeks from Rebellion."

"No other explanation." Amelia begins crying.

"Don't." I gather her to me. The touch of another human, a woman, stirs me deeply. I have missed Diana. I have missed intimacy.

Amelia dries her eyes on her shirttail and hands Joseph a cookie. He's ignoring our conversation and tears—in his own little world. He's eighteen-months old now and walking. Talking some.

"Are we going back for her?" she asks me.

"We can't. Too dangerous for you and Joseph."

"You can't let Thor raise his daughter. He'll destroy her."

"I know, and I won't."

"Let's get on the right trail and continue on to Bethel." Amelia hops to her feet. "I will care for Joseph while you go back for her."

I think about what that will entail. I will see my father first. Talk to Dahlia and tell her the truth. Then leave the village again.

*Dear Jesus, what kind of pilgrimage am I on?*

# 375 ACR

## 36

**"WHAT ARE YOU READING?"** Tanya asks me as I close the diary belonging to my great-great grandfather, David Goldman. What a rich story! His life was like a pirate's portrayed in a novel. David lived in a wilderness two centuries before Brent was born, yet travelled half way across the world to meet with King Jesus and worship him.

Tanya is fourteen. Brent Goldman is a year older. They attend the same Christian Academy in Jupiter. Brent's grandfather was Joseph Goldman, David's only son. Brent married a woman named Susan, and they had two children, a son and daughter. Their daughter Cynthia married young and died during childbirth while Brent's father Charles lived to be in his eighties. Every new generation of the Goldman's have recorded their family history. Cory Lindsey was the first in that lineage. He was married to Mary Taylor, a famous female evangelist who openly opposed the ruling Antichrist. Brent's legacy is one of bravery.

He wonders if it's his time to make this difficult journey to Jerusalem. Someone from his town must bow before Jesus once a year, or rain will not fall in their area. But, after reading his grandfather's account of all the dangers and heartaches he'd face, Brent questions if he has what it takes to make the journey. David went at age sixteen.

"Why don't you let me read that diary?" Tanya asks.

"Maybe another time." Brent stows the diary on a bookshelf at his house. Since Christ's return, the earth has become more populated. Many people accept Christ as God's only Son, but others congregate in communities and rebel against His rule. From studying the Bible, Brent knows that Satan will be released from his prison near the end of the Millennium and bring an army against King Jesus' rule.

Jesus will win that final war. Satan, his demons, and those not redeemed by the holy blood of Jesus will be judged and sentenced to the eternal fire of Hell. Then Jesus will turn over his authority to God who will judge the unsaved dead. Afterwards, the former world will pass away and a new one that is perfect will be created. As in the Garden of Eden, there will be no night, no need for the River of Life to produce trees with healing fruit for medicines to heal the sick. No death. Only eternal life for the born-again. Brent won't live long enough to see the end, but like his father, grandfather, and his great-great-grandfather David Goldman, he wants to find his place in history and eventually into the pages of the Goldman's Diary. It's his destiny.

"I'm going to hold you to that promise, Brent," Tanya says.

"How about some dessert? Mom made a chocolate pie."

"Sounds good to me."

Tanya leaves mid-afternoon, so Brent has time to lay down and rest on the sofa while he envisions what David Goldman's life was like. It is 173 ACR in the timetable of history. Brent can almost see David as he faced off with his one true love, Dahlia. Was he shocked at seeing her pregnant and married to his best friend, Milo? What a scene. . .

"You're back," Dahlia says as David approaches her front porch.

"Yes, my father told me you had married." He sits in the swing and gently pushes it into motion with a foot. "When are you due?"

"In a few months," Dahlia replies. "Are you mad?"

"No, there is much you do not know about my life."

Dahlia frowns. "Tell me, David. All of it."

And he does—from the time he met the ship captain Benjamin to the time Diana the prostitute gave birth to his son, Joseph.

Brent imagines David facing off with Thor when he travelled to Rebellion to get Diana's daughter Samantha back. He had not gone to the sinful village alone. He paid some strong men to help him.

David won that fight. Thor was dead when David returned to Bethel with Sam. By then, his father Joseph had died from a lung disease. No mention of Milo or Dahlia again in the diary.

David lived in his father's house, never married, and home-schooled his children until they were grown. Soon after Joe had turned eighteen and graduated high school, and Sam married her sweetheart, David packed up and left Bethel, planning to return to Jerusalem.

Only a few letters arrived from David in the following months. Then nothing. Possibly, he died. The rest of his life story remains a mystery. Why didn't he return home? Did he make it to Jerusalem?

# 695 ACR

## 37

**GENERATIONS OF GOLDMAN'S** have passed off the pages of time. Mary Ann Johnson has a collection of diaries that have been passed down in her family from father to son, mother to daughter, etc. Her mother was a Goldman, but she'd married a Johnson. That did not make Mary feel any less a Goldman. She treasured the twelve diaries in her family collection. Since Christ's return, the world had changed. In only seven centuries, small communities had become large cities. Rural roads were paved to connect smaller villages. Technology was rediscovered, so human communication had taken a giant leap. Satellites circling the earth supported the use of individual cellphones.

Mary is an astronomer by trade. She studies the stars—actually the universe. As a Christian, she believes that Jesus Christ once walked the earth as a human being. Not any less God, He is part of the Godhead referred to as the Holy Trinity. She also knows there is an unholy trinity—Satan, the False Prophet, and the Antichrist. For now, they have been locked away from influencing evil upon humankind.

For seven years before Jesus returned, the unholy trinity had ruled the earth. But God had commanded the planet to rebel against Satan's authority. He'd sent two Old Testament prophets back to earth to oversee the fulfillment of biblical prophecy. Moses and Elijah reeked horror on humankind and the natural earth. People suffered for their sins against humankind, their unbelief in Jesus. Eventually, the Battle of Armageddon between good and evil occurred. Cities crumbled and fires burnt out much of modern society. The landscape changed.

Then Jesus returned to set up His Kingdom. That is the Kingdom Mary resides in. She wonders what Jesus would have her do now that she is twenty-seven and has earned a doctorate in her field of astronomy. She is not married; still devoted to her parents as an only child. She prays daily and reads the Scriptures religiously. She waits for instructions from the Almighty. She is a Goldman. That's huge.

The story about the cabin in the wilderness puzzles Mary. David Goldman had been to Jerusalem to worship Jesus. He'd been ousted off a boat over five-hundred years ago on his way home to Bethel in Brazil with his two young children—Samantha, Thor's daughter, and Joseph, his biological son birthed by a prostitute named Diana.

Diana had died in childbirth. Two women serving as paid nannies had abandoned David during the long journey from Israel to Brazil. The Widow Young he met in Jamestown, Brazil, took over their roles.

Then Thor from Rebellion had sent men to kidnap his daughter, Sam. David, with the Widow Young and his two children escaped harm, but the boat captain kicked them off his sailing vessel.

They were left alone on the banks of a river to face the Wilderness. David prayed and they walked. They stumbled upon a new cabin on the side of a mountain. No one was home. Who built the cabin, stocked it, then left it for them to winter there for three months?

No explanation had been given in David's diary. The answer must be squirreled away in someone else's family diary.

Come spring, an angel named Dutch guided David's family through the mountainous terrain. They soon encountered two men owning a raft floating down a rushing river. Dutch asked the men to take the family the rest of their way home. They agreed, so Dutch left.

Sawyer and Jason let the family off their raft within miles of Bethel. David had talked much in his diary about loving a woman named Dahlia. He had been betrothed to her before leaving for Israel at age sixteen. Mary could only imagine Dahlia's shock when David had returned home to Bethel with a nanny and two children to raise.

Mary had never encountered an angel, though it was said they rarely left Jerusalem anymore. Why was that? Was it lack of faith on the part of people living outside of Israel? She prayed that wasn't her.

She badly wanted a divine experience with Jesus. For a while, she'd thought about traveling to Jerusalem. What is her destiny?

Mary left the Kitt Peak National Observatory, fifty-six miles south of Tuscan, Arizona. Her grandparents had returned to America from Brazil when they learned a warming trend had occurred in the Northern Hemisphere. Grandpa Julien Goldman had a hankering to pan for gold, so he believed the West was the place to live. Ophelia, his wife, never questioned Julien's wisdom when it came to life.

Mary laughs at the thought. She needs to get a life for herself and quit dwelling on the past. She'd been reading too many of the family diaries for the past three years. It was warping her life. There seemed to be only hours for work, reading, and sleep on her agenda.

The curvy road down the mountain leads to a small community called Locus—no idea who gave it that name. She owns a small apartment in a three-story building that once was a bakery. It's almost as if she can smell the bread baked into the stucco that frames her apartment. On her way home, she stops to buy groceries.

"Good afternoon, Mary," Gray says as he stows her milk, juice, and fresh fruit in a paper grocery bag. "How were the stars today?"

"Unyielding," she replies, smiling at the grocery-store owner. He can't be more than thirty-five—she's heard his wife recently died.

"As to be expected." He nods his head.

"Thank you, Gray. I'll see you in a few days."

Mary turns to leave when he calls out her name.

"Hey, are you busy on Saturday?"

She turns around. "What's Saturday?"

"My day off. I thought you might show me your observatory."

Mary is surprised at Gray's offer. Is he asking for a date?

"How about it? I'm a stargazer, too."

She laughs. "All you need to do is go outside your house and look up at night, Gray. There are plenty of stars in Arizona skies."

He winks, an elbow on the counter. "Not the same as looking at the stars with you." Not a muscle moves. Her turn.

Mary feels her cheeks flush. "Okay. I'll let you know a time."

"I'll look forward to a lesson in astronomy."

Mary hurriedly leaves, thinking Gray wants more than that from her. Is that how Granny Ophelia got hoodwinked by Grandpa Julien?

She cannot remember when she's last had a date. "Jesus! Am I in trouble?" slips from her lips as she puts her groceries in the car.

# 38

## Saturday

**THE SUN SET HOURS** ago as Mary anxiously stares out of the window of her apartment at the street below. Already late in April, the weather is pleasantly cool at this hour. Before the night ends, the temps will drop into the forties—too chilly for comfort. Her date is late.

She wonders if Gray has stood her up. She's not a pretty woman, a bit too thin for failing to eat meals when busy with her work.

But Gray is not perfect, either. He'd lost the lower portion of one leg in a fall off a cliff. She'd read about his accident in the newspaper last year, but no explanation was given as to why he'd fallen.

*Mmm* . . . Lost in that thought, Mary spies Gray's Ford truck pulling into a parking space below her. She watches as he gets out, using a cane to steady himself although he has a prosthetic leg.

During the past two-hundred years technology had taken a giant leap, primarily due to the massive amounts of literature left behind in titanic tubes that were virtually indestructible by fire. And there had been many fires during the Battle of Armageddon. The world had been up sided, civilization nearly destroyed. But some people survived.

Like her ancestors. And Brent's.

During a time of great tribulation, massive numbers of Jews had travelled across continents and settled in Israel in anticipation of Jesus' return. Some world citizens became reborn by grace because of their trust in the grace of God and the belief that Jesus is God's only Son.

The Goldman's dwelled outside of Israel in the Wilderness. The land was raw and unyielding back then, offering little conveniences for humans or animals. But vegetation recovered during the first century of Christ's rule. Villages grew into towns. Cities eventually flourished.

Finally, the forests thickened with tall hardwoods and pines, providing seeds as food for the growing population of animals. Water sources cleared and became usable for human consumption. Schools began to educate children again. Technology came into play.

Mary was a direct descendant of Cory and Mary Lindsey, too many generations back to count. She was named from Mary, her great grandmother to the tenth-degree. She smiles while observing Gray.

"I will never heal someone by my shadow," Mary utters as there is a knock at the door. "Coming!" she calls out to greet her date.

Opening the door feels like opening a new future. Seeing Gray lights up her eyes and troubles her heart that she cares so much.

*Will he hurt me, like the last man I loved?*

"I hope you're ready for a great adventure!" Gray hawks, stomping his cane on the wood floor, startling Mary to the present.

"It is you that will be astounded, my friend."

He grins. "Is that all we are?"

"Of course, we're friends." Mary gathers her wrap and purse in preparation to leave. "What?" She notices he's staring.

"You! No star can match that smile."

Mary laughs. "I heard you had a silver tongue."

"No one pays any attention to rumors."

"I do." Mary steadies herself for a moment.

"Shall we go and talk about all that stuff in the truck?"

"All what?"

"Friendship. Silver tongues." He laughs.

Mary observes Gray cautiously. He's let his blond hair grow shoulder-length. His eyes are a dark coffee color. He's as handsome as any actor on the movie screen, so she wonders what he's doing dating her. The scars on her right cheek aren't pretty. The house fire that killed her younger sister left Mary alive but severely scarred. Her parents had denied reconstructive surgery due to the expense. Only Mary's bright blue eyes were left for any semblance of beauty. She's been told they sparkled like the stars in the universe. Mary Lindsey was said to have had the same attribute. Only, her face was perfect.

"You don't know much about me." Gray broke the silence as he opened the door for Mary. "But I know a great deal about you."

She blushes. "How? We've barely spoken at the grocery store."

"People come in and out, buy stuff, and talk. I listen."

"Okay . . . so what do people say about me?"

They exit her apartment building and approach his truck. He opens the passenger door for Mary and helps her inside.

"I know you are single. And that you were once engaged."

"And that was a disaster!" Mary exclaims with a laugh.

He lingers, holding on to the passenger door.

"You broke it off with the guy, why?"

"I realized I was not what Doyle needed."

"Care to explain?"

"Get in the truck, and I'll think about it."

He walks around the front of the Ford and mounts the driver's seat. When his door is shut, I say, "I'm sorry your wife died."

"She was pregnant with our first child," Gray reveals.

"That was not in the news report."

"I asked the paper to leave it out, for Joy's parents' sake."

Mary nods. She likes this guy. He's honest. Doyle was not honest with Mary about why he'd asked her to marry him. But that was all in the past now. She did not want to think about that tonight.

"Are you going to tell me why you broke up with Doyle?"

"Save it for another time. I have a question for you."

"Shoot!" He takes a curve up the mountain fast and Mary falls his way. "Sit close, I can hear you better since the wind's kicked up."

"A storm is coming. We might not be able to see the stars."

Gray puts his arm around Mary. "I'll watch the stars in your eyes."

* * *

Mary woke up the next morning in her bed, thinking about last night. When they got to the observatory, it was storming cats and dogs outdoors. All she could see through the telescope were dark clouds.

Gray looked through the telescope, then grinned. "Perfect."

She'd pushed him away and looked through the lens. "I don't see anything but clouds." She looked at him. "What did you see?"

"You. That's why I came up here."

"He kissed me," Mary utters as she gets out of bed. "He doesn't care that my face is scarred. But I wonder if he has another agenda."

# 39

**THEY HAD BEEN DATING** three months. It was already into August and people were gathering what they'd need for a hard winter ahead. Arizona usually cooled off in October due to its many open spaces, mountains, and deserts. People relied on burning wood in fireplaces since the electric grid was unreliable. People who still wanted climate control—what a laugh! —had passed laws to limit the use of oil and gas. Ugly windmills that killed birds had been erected in the desert.

Gray was coming over tonight after he closed his grocery store to ask Mary something. Was he going to propose? She loved him. But had never determined if he had an ulterior motive in wooing her.

She'd purchased a new sweater with woolen pants to wear on their date. Tonight, they were driving into a larger city called Alpaca. He'd reserved a table at a fancy Mexican restaurant for their late supper.

The drive takes an hour. Gray talks about his plans to build a new home in the spring. He already has an architect working on it. Mary listens, wondering if she'll be living in that house by next summer.

The meal is great, as promised. The spices flavoring the food are grown in a hothouse behind the restaurant. They polish off their meal with a sopapillas, crisp fritters drizzled with cinnamon and honey.

Lifestyles are healthier and more natural in the millennium. No preservatives in growing foods means less cancer incidents. Smoking is unpopular among the young. And there are few drugs available.

Why make the same mistakes as residents of the former world?

"You said you had a surprise for me," Mary says as they get into Gray's truck to start home. "Are you going to keep me in suspense?"

He removes an envelope from his pocket. "Here. You'll see."

"What is this?" She opens the envelope and spies two airplane tickets. "I don't understand." Blue eyes wandered to Gray.

"Will you go with me to Jerusalem to see the King?"

*What?* Mary realizes the question was only a thought.

"I see I've surprised you." He laughs.

Mary is speechless, joy flooding her spirit.

"We can be married in the Holy City. Please say yes."

*Marry?* No words form on her lips.

"I take that to be a yes!" Gray pulls the truck over to the side of the road and reaches for Mary. His kiss is firm and seals the deal.

Mary listens to Gray's plan as they drive home. They will be in Jerusalem in late September to enter the Temple and visit with King Jesus. It is a dream Mary never expected to fulfill. A trip to Israel.

And I am going to marry Gray.

* * *

Mary cannot wait to get inside her apartment and phone her parents with the good news. They will be as surprised as she had. But this proposal was more than marriage. It was an opportunity to appear before King Jesus Himself. They would first fly into Cairo, Egypt later this month and go through the qualification process required before travelling on the Holy Highway to Jerusalem. Only the pure in heart, saved by grace, can behold the healing trees lining the River or Life.

It is a bit late in the day, still Mary phones. Her mother always has her cellphone on—a habit she cannot break even during sleep.

"Mama! It's Mary. Am I calling too late?"

"I was asleep, dear."

"Sorry, but I have urgent news."

"You got a promotion at the observatory?"

"No, Mama. I got engaged tonight," Mary gushes.

There is silence at the other end of the line.

"Mama? Did I lose you?"

"Mary, you never said you were dating anyone."

"I did, Mama. I told you I met Gray at the grocery store and he asked me out. Three months ago. Don't you remember?"

"I do, but you've said nothing since about this Gray person."

"Gray Simpson, Mama. His last name is Simpson."

Mary realizes she's a bit perturbed at her mother for sounding so displeased at her announcement. "You'll like him."

"So, you say. How long have you been dating?"

"Love has no time table, Mama. We love each other."

Silence becomes even louder and more disturbing.

"Are you sure Gray is the right person for you?"

127

"Mama, nobody has asked me out on a date since I broke up with Doyle. That was seven years ago. Why can't you be happy for me?"

"Well, you know . . ."

"Yes, I know . . . I am scarred in the face. I am not a pretty woman. I'm smart and witty—doesn't that count for something?"

"Don't marry this man until your father and I meet him."

"Is that an ultimatum, Mama? Do I need your permission to marry at twenty-seven? The wedding won't cost you a penny."

"And why is that? Doesn't he want a public wedding?"

"We are getting married in Jerusalem, in late September."

Silence, again.

"I just wanted you to know, Mama. Please tell Daddy."

Mary ends the call and sits down on the sofa. Then cries.

# 40

**"YOU KNOW WHY THE** East Gate is so important," Gray tells me. "Weren't you paying attention to our teacher in Cairo?"

"Ezekiel, chapter 43," I reply. "The Prophet Ezekiel had a vision of Jesus coming from the east. His voice was like the roar of mighty waters and the earth shone with His glory."

Gray adds, "God's spirit led Ezekiel to the exact place where the glory of the Lord entered the Temple that faced east. Jesus said to Ezekiel, 'Son of man, this is the place of My throne and the place for the soles of My feet, where I will dwell among the Israelites forever."

Gray falls silent, a smile on his handsome face.

"The Jaffa Gate!" I exclaim. "It was the first gate built as an entrance to the city of Jerusalem. As promised the Twelve Disciples, when Christ returned to earth at the end of the Tribulation, He stepped down on the Temple Mount and walked to the East Gate."

"The Gate of Mercy, or the Golden Gate."

I cannot help from chuckling. "You've been testing me, my love."

"Just checking. Wouldn't want you to enter the East Gate and get in trouble," he says. "Our group is scheduled to enter the Temple through the North Gate on the first day of the Festival of Booths, exactly five days after *Yom Kippur* ends—or the Day of Atonement. We will be greeted by the Prince himself, and tour the Temple before our appointed time with Jesus  Then exit through the South Gate."

"My ancestor, David Goldman, did the opposite," I share.

Gray tilts his head to one side. "Why are you so fascinated with a man who lived over five-hundred years ago?  It doesn't add up."

"It does to me." We trail our group leader up the steep stairs that takes us one plateau closer to our destination as we ascend the mountain and approach the Temple where Jesus dwells.

Gray sits on a rock. "I'm out of breath."

I stand next to him, panting. Several people in our group are sweating from the arduous climb. Our leader, an angel who appears to be human, never seems to run out of energy. I still have human form, but one day I will be changed into something immortal and everlasting.

"We'll camp there for the night," Golan declares.

"Thank God!" I declare and drop to my butt on the grass.

The crescent moon is rising on the eastern horizon casting a glow over the rich growth of greenery decorating every plateau on this side of the mountain. I feel so privileged to be engaged to Gray and on our way to actually bow before Jesus, the co-creator of our beautiful planet in conjunction with God and the Holy Spirit. The Trinity. All for One, and One for All. I consider the uniqueness of their divine existence.

Golan instructs his assistants to set up tents for our group that includes thirty humans from all over the globe. Gray and I are the only Americans in our group. We'd spent the past two months in Cairo, Egypt, learning how to behave inside the Temple. We were warned not to ask the angels questions. That they were here to study us; not us to study them. I slept in a tent with six other females.

Although we are from different countries and speak in our native languages, we understood one another. It is one of the miracles of the Holy Land. People here are healthy and live to be very old. A canopy of light hovers over the city during nights. Jerusalem is often called "The City of Lights." The temperature is always comfortable.

King Jesus meets with visitors inside the temple's Holy of Holies. He calls us the "Redeemed" because have been cleansed of all sin by His blood through God's grace. As I soak in the peaceful atmosphere, I think upon all I have seen and learned during my journey.

Soon, my eyelids grow heavy and I sleep dreamlessly as if floating on a cloud. I cannot imagine how tomorrow will be more perfect.

* * *

We are up early the next morning. Breakfast is served. The juice is sweet and coffee never tasted better. Golan told us that the crispy flakes coated in honey were made just like the manna Jehovah God dropped from Heaven to feed the wandering Israelites in the Sinai Desert after Moses led them out of Egypt slavery. We are advised not to save any manna since the flaky cakes will be no good tomorrow. So, I eat my fair share. No worms for me. I have never tasted a breakfast so satisfying, but this is the closest to Heaven on Earth as I've been.

Gray and I are scheduled to enter the Holy of Holies and visit with Jesus sometime mid-afternoon. Golan is not certain of the exact time since Jesus determines how much time He has with each visitor.

I have a few questions I want to ask. Nothing about angels. Of course, I will bow before King Jesus, worship and thank Him for my salvation. But, I'm curious about one particular member of my family.

While climbing the stairs up the mountain to the Temple, I spy some of the Old Testament prophets in deep discussion. I can only imagine how they are comparing the Word of God given to them back in Old-Testament days with the modern-day fulfilled prophecies.

I would love to be a little bird on a nearby branch listening in.

We finally arrive outside the Temple late morning, but we cannot yet enter the Temple. Golan has food delivered for our lunch as we sit in five circles on the green grass to eat a well-deserved meal.

My anticipation of facing King Jesus is growing. And my fear.

"Perfect love casts out fear," Gray reminds me, holding tightly to my hand. "Love, you will do fine. Just don't ask too many questions."

He dottles his head as if he is teasing.

But I know he is not. I am full of questions.

FULL!

# 41

## Last Friday in September

**OUR ANGELIC LEADER, GOLAN**, tells us that the Prince himself is here to greet all groups entering the Temple today. I cannot contain my excitement. Since I was a little girl my parents talked of visiting Jerusalem, but they never did. They did not have the funds for an airline ticket, and with the responsibilities of family and work, just failed to fulfill a desire. I was fortunate to meet Gray, become engaged, since he funded our trip and we planned to marry while in Jerusalem.

We are lined up outside the Temple at the north entrance. Below us is a colorful array of tents set up on multiple plateaus that look like large steps to the base from my point of view. Today, like all others, is beautiful. A continual mist rises from the ground each morning, and the Cloud of Mercy hangs over the city until noon each day providing enough moisture without rain falling. It's a mystery the meteorologists long to solve. Good luck with that! I chuckle to myself.

"What's so funny?" Gray nudges me on the shoulder.

"Oh, I don't know . . . everything is wonderful, don't you think?"

"Yes. Perfect in every way. Too bad the world outside does not get totally with the program." He steps forward as the line moves.

"At this rate, we won't get inside the Temple till mid-afternoon," I complain for the first time. "Sorry." I repent.

"When the cloud lifts at noon it will become hotter standing out here," Gray notes. "But I came prepared." He opens an umbrella.

I laugh hard. "I knew there was a reason I'm marrying you."

"Which is only in two days. Sunday, at 2 p.m."

"I don't need a reminder, Gray. Take me to the church on time."

He laughs. "I never saw your humor when you came into the grocery store to shop," Gray expresses. "You are a surprise."

"Yeah, a star-gazer with humor!" I exclaim. "Imagine."

Water bottles are passed out among our group as one p.m. approaches. Gray raises his umbrella, but he's not the only one. As a result, the line separates to allow for the inconvenience of the shading.

Gray and I enter the Temple at 3:35 p.m. I am exhausted, but running the adrenalin of excitement. The Prince politely bows.

"Prime Minister." I shake his strong, firm hand.

"Welcome to the Holy City, and the Temple."

"Thank you. This is my fiancé Gray," I introduce him. "We are to be married at Saint Gabriel's Chapel on Sunday."

"Congratulations to both of you."

We trail Golan inside the Temple. The Great Hall is 35 x 70 feet. Inside the portico gate for the animal sacrifices are two tables. Burnt, sin, and restitution offerings, are still periodically offered as a worship to King Jesus. Jewish tradition continues for another two-hundred years—until the time of judgment when sinners face consequences.

There are rooms for the singers and priests. The Temple has three stories above the Great Hall. I suppose where the Twelve live. I wonder if Gray and I will have the opportunity to greet Moses himself.

What about the Disciple John?

"What are you thinking, love?" Gray whispers as we continue our tour. "You've been unusually quiet. Mesmerized, I'd say."

"Exactly!" I smile, but my thoughts remain private.

We are shown to a room where we wait to be called inside the Holy of Holies to meet with King Jesus. I think of the time Satan occupied that space in protest to God's choice of a Son. Satan was deposed in Heaven and cast out with his rebellious angels when he tried to subject God to his servitude. That didn't go well at all.

It is 4:16 when my name comes up. I touch Gray's shoulder for reassurance, then walk cautiously into the room where Jesus sits.

It's not a throne, but a white-stone bench. I notice that hay has been scattered across the shimmering golden floor. *The manger?*

"Yes," Jesus says, "I like to be reminded that my humble beginnings started in a cave in Bethlehem and Mother Mary placed me in a manger where sheep were fed with hay. That is why I call my people 'sheep', and myself their Shepherd. How are you today, Mary."

"Good! No, great!" I exclaim, then bow to worship Jesus.

He reaches out for my hand. "Come sit next to me. I understand you have questions you want to ask me." He smiles.

"How did you know?" I am startled.

He laughs. "Not much gets passed me."

I am surprised Jesus speaks like a normal person. Does that change with each generation? What about in Moses' time?

"Yes, I am changeless in many ways, but I enjoy talking to my people on their level of understanding. It gives me joy."

I smile. "You are more than I hoped for, Lord!"

He puts an arm around my shoulder and hugs me.

"Now, what do you want to know about David Goldman?"

Surprise is on the tip of my tongue. "What happened to him after he left Bethel? The family diary said nothing of him afterwards."

"Why, he came here, to see me again," Jesus replies then picks up a wooden cross lying next to him on the bench. "He made this."

"He was a carpenter," I recall.

"Yes, like me. And lost as to what he was to do with the rest of his life when He visited me. The love of his life, Dahlia, had married his best friend by the time he returned home. And, of course, his wife Diana had given birth to Thor's daughter. And Little Joseph, but died during birthing him. David made it home, but never married—had trouble keeping nannies working for him. A truly troubled soul."

By then, I am weeping. "So, David remained in Jerusalem."

"Yes, and opened a carpenter shop where he spent the rest of his life creating religious symbols to sell to visitors who came here."

"Gold Religious Symbols."

"Yes. Created by David. His work is displayed all over the world today. He is famous. And blessed. He will rise on the Last Day."

It's a lot for me to take in, so I am quiet.

"What can I do for you today, Mary? Something personal."

"Just bless me, Lord, that I might live my life worthily."

# 42

**"OH . . .!" PEOPLE SHADE** their eyes as I exit the door to the Holy of Holies.  "What's wrong?" I shout.  "Did I miss something?"

"Your face, honey," Gray says in a whisper.  "It's glowing."

I suddenly realized the room is bright as I touch my warm face.

"I'm glowing?" I utter, astonished.

"Yes, like the face of Moses!" a woman exclaims.

"Here." Golan hands me a mask.  "Cover your glory."

"Why?" I accept the mask, paralyzed for a moment.

"Here, I'll help you."  Golan attaches the face mask.

I move to a corner, people parting like the Red Sea for Moses, although I have no staff to order anything.  I actually snicker.

"People do not need to see the glory of God," Golan says.

"Why?  It's not like I have the plague."

"You might.  The Glory of God spotlights sin.  Who knows what these people have done since they left Egypt.  Who know their sinful thoughts.  Only God, only Jesus, only the Holy Spirit."

I sober at the thought.  "I might strike them dead?"

He nods.  "One person who received the glory did."

"How long shall I wear the mask?" I inquire.

He shakes his head.  "Only you can decide that."

Gray is shaken when I finally find my way over to his side.  "Isn't it your turn to go inside?"  I look up at him through the holes in my mask.  "Please don't miss this opportunity to meet with Jesus, Gray."

"I let two people go in before me.  Mind waiting?"

"No."  I touch the mask, wondering what wonders will happen to me as the glory of God rests on my face.  My face.  Imagine!

* * *

Gray and I are at the base of the mountain by eight o'clock, a radiant moon lighting the pathway that leads into Jerusalem. Golan has arranged for our group to stay in a hotel downtown.  Our group will tour the city tomorrow, on Saturday.  Then be married on Sunday.  We have tickets to fly home to Tuscan, Arizona on Monday.

# 43

## Sunday

**ALREADY THE FIRST OF OCTOBER,** I am marrying Gray Henry Simpson today, a man I love dearly and respect. He's a fine Christian whose first wife died. We met at his grocery store a few blocks from the apartment complex where I live. He was always kind and helpful when I shopped for food. Plus, he's ignored the hideous scar on my cheek left by a housefire. Rather, he chooses to see the positives.

My respect for others, my intellectual pursuits and my faith in Christ. I love him for his honesty. Still, I'm a bit apprehensive about removing the covering to my face. It's time. Yet I haven't. Why is that?

Deep down, it's because I do not know what to expect. Has my image changed because of the glory? All I know is that I've been a main attraction in Jerusalem. People follow me. Well, me and Gray, like we are celebrities. In a way, I suppose we are. I've been told that few people receive the glory as I have. A miracle. And people wonder.

We arrived at Saint Gabriel's Chapel an hour ago. I am in the Bride's Dressing Room, while Gray occupies the Groom's. A beautiful wedding dress and veil has been provided—complements of the fee Gray paid the manager for our privilege of saying our wedding vows in this beautiful setting. And I do mean beautiful. The floors are white marble with flecks of gold. The furniture in the bride's room is cherry with plush red upholstery. I stand before a ceiling-to-floor length mirror and view my pristine image in white—except for the dark mask.

*Jesus,* I whisper to myself, *should I take it off?*

I wait for an answer. None comes. He's depending on me to decide, so I will. The mask will stay on till Gray takes it off my face.

*Then we will both see what I look like.*

I hear a knock on the door. "Yes?" I answer.

The door cracks open and a dark man in a suit steps inside. He's Egyptian, I think. Very tall and thin. And he's not smiling.

"Is it time? I mean, for our ceremony?"

"Momentarily," he replies, looking elegant in his black suit worn with a white shirt and blood-red bowtie. "I came to warn you."

For a second, my heart skips beats.

"Did the groom skip out on me?"

He chuckles. His smile is comforting and refreshing. "No ma'am, he's as anxious as a rooster about to crow and wake up the morning."

I smile. Interesting analogy.

"So, warn me."

"You have many guests," he states.

"I don't know anyone here. This is a private wedding. I don't even have bridesmaids or a flower girl!" I exclaim. "Who's here?"

"Everyone that can squeeze into the chapel," he replies.

I am astounded. "Why?"

"To see your face, of course. When you remove the mask."

"Oh." I touch my face. It feels hot, probably from wearing the heavy beaded wedding dress and white satin shoes too tight for my size eight feet. "Okay," I say. "What does the priest think?"

"The wedding will happen on schedule."

"Good."

I hear the organ music as the Wedding March fills the chapel outside the door. My heart stutters, then I stand tall.

"Then, Sir, I should go and fulfill my duty to the groom."

He opens the door for me. "Have a good life."

But, his words fall on deaf ears as I start down the aisle toward the altar where Gray stands like a Greek God he's so beautiful. And here I am, the ugly duckling, the Cinderella who lost a shoe, plain Jane in American terms, about to marry a dreamboat only Disney imagines.

The crowd stuffed in the pews glare at me. I think in a hundred years they will all be dust blowing in the streets of Jerusalem. Or trapped in boxes six feet under. Held there till Judgment Day.

Gray takes my hand as I step up to the altar next to him. His hand is warm and comforting. We will have a good life. I'm joyful.

A kind woman seated on the first-row steps over to receive the small bouquet of red roses I carry. I turn slightly and thank her.

The minister clears his throat and looks us both in the eye.

*This is it,* I think.  A marriage my parents' scorn.  They believe Gray is not good enough for me.  I think otherwise.

"Ladies and Gentlemen, we are gathered here today to witness the marriage of these two fine Christians from America . . ."

I am so excited about marrying Gray, the minister's words are nearly lost to me.  But, thank Jesus, I knew when to say "I do".

"I now pronounce you man and wife," the minister declares.  "Gray, you may remove the veil to your wife's face and kiss her."

I close my eyes in anticipation.  I feel the veil lift.  Then hear a thump—which makes me open my eyes.  Gray is lying on the floor, passed out.  People are screaming and phone cameras are snapping photos of the scheme.  I have no idea what is going on. None. Zilch.

# 999 ACR

## 44

**"DO YOU REALLY EXPECT** the world as we know it to end in eleven months?" Donald Pinson asks his wife, Rebecca."

"Do I believe the sun will come up tomorrow?" she responds.

"You know what I mean, Becca. You're not stupid."

Becca sighs. "I wish I could say the same for you, dear."

They celebrated their first anniversary on January 1. Twelve days ago. It appears that love blinded her to the true identity of Don.

"I'm a realist, Becca—far from stupid," he asserts.

Becca spreads her hands. "Why are we arguing over a well-known fact? Jesus said He would give people a thousand years to decide which side they were on. Satan's or His. I know where I stand." She glares at him. "Apparently, you don't. Since you've bought into a fantasy."

Don continues to get dressed. He has an appointment with Dr. George Morose, renowned creationist's expert who has scorned the idea of the Bible's view of the story of how life on earth began.

"Surely, you can't support Dr. Morose's wild-haired theory that evolution is the explanation of how we as homo sapiens got here?" Becca argues her point. "God our Creator made the world in six days."

Don scowls, his scathing look upsetting Becca even more.

"Don, I love you. You know that. Please don't go on national BBC and support this man's theory to discount the Holy Bible."

Becca is worried that Don's disobedience will hinder those who are new to trusting in Jesus. Time is running out for decisions.

Don is disgusted at Becca. He actually believed she'd come around to support his belief in the natural evolution of humankind. Ignoring her stare, he straightens his silk tie while observing his image staring back at him in the floor-length mirror. Then turns to her.

"Jesus doesn't have the power to end the world."

Becca is stunned. Don has no inkling of what is true.

"You're wrong, Donald. Just because Jesus is kind and merciful and doesn't force His will upon people is not an indication He's any less powerful.  God put earth in His hands. He loves everyone equally. The sinner and the believer.  But God has His rules, too."

"What does that mean, Becca?"

"It means I'm right and you're wrong," she claims. "You'd realize the Bible is true, Don, if you'd only read the New Testament."

He checks in the mirror to see if his thick dark hair is in place.  He doesn't want to continue arguing his point this morning when he's due at the television station in forty-five minutes.  But he can't help it.

"What about the flood?" Becca stands behind him.

Don spins around.  "What flood?  Has it been on the news?"

Becca walks a few steps and sits down on the bed, hands folded in her lap. Don is due at the television station and this conversation is too complicated to finish in one session—not that their view on faith haven't been discussed over the past year. Her father, Kilmer Golden, had warned that two people of different beliefs are incompatible

It appears he was right. Is there a meeting ground?

"What flood?" Don demands.  "Keep it short, I need to go."

"The Great Flood," she replies.

He shakes his head.  "Can this wait until I get home tonight?"

By this time, tears cloud Becca's eyes. "Yes, but I want to show you something.  Promise you'll see my DVD before revolting?"

He chuckles.  "More Christian propaganda?"

"Good luck with your interview," she concludes the discussion. "You have to go, and I need to dress now or I'll be late for class."

Don kisses her on the forehead then leaves for the station.

This is not the way Becca expected their first year of marriage to unfold. A year ago, they'd made promises. To love each other, but obedience had been removed from the script since Don believed in equity. She'd seen nothing positive in continuing their discussion.

Becca read the time on her cell phone. She needed to hurry.

The drive over to Emory University takes thirty minutes in decent traffic. This morning a parking lot of cars are on the move She uses her keycard to get in the building and finds her assigned classroom. She's teaching World Religion this semester, so the precepts of

Christianity are included She'd researched a number of related materials over the holidays. Everything she'd read confirmed the authenticity of the Bible. In response, her faith had grown exponentially. But produced worry over the condition of Don's soul.

She needed for him to trust in Jesus, be forgiven of his sin, and live eternally in Heaven with her. The two worldviews of how the universe came into existence were at odds. The Big Bang Theory supported the theory that the universe, it's stars and planets, took billions of years to evolve into some kind of system of natural order. When the physical conditions on earth were perfect, signs of life appeared in the ocean. In another billion or so years one-celled plants evolved into a humanoid, eventually becoming *homo sapiens.*

This scientific view discounts God's involvement with creation. Don believes in evolution. Becca doesn't. The biblical view supports a Supreme Creator, a single entity with the power to design the whole system. Jesus, God's Son, was uniquely involved in the process of creation. Through His physical birth and sacrificial death on a Roman cross, God through grace granted forgiveness for sin perpetrated on Adam and Eve's offspring. Bible history confirms this view.

Yet, the argument continues between Christians and atheists.

Becca had known before agreeing to marry Don that he was a Jew. Blinded by love, they'd never talked in depth about faith. The last person to accept the authenticity of the Torah, the first five books of the Old Testament, was Don's great-grandfather. His sons rejected belief in any god. Generations of unbelief followed this legacy.

The Bible states the sins of the father are visited upon the third and fourth generations. Don has never read the Bible. If he'd studied the Old Testament, he would know that God favored the Israelites. He would know that Jesus is the Messiah prophets of Old foretold, that He came first for the Jews—to show them The Way of peace. But Don hasn't. In Becca's naïve way of thinking, she believed she could convince Don to view history the truthful way. So far, she had failed.

But not given up.  No, she loved Don far too much.

✳ ✳ ✳

Don arrives at the television station thirty minutes before he's due to appear on air with Dr. George Morose. His newest book release is

141

entitled: "The Priesthood of Humankind." He advocates that there is no God and that every person has god-hood buried in their genetics. They are masters of their own destiny. Born with the ability to control their circumstances. The idea a divine king rules over the world from the Jerusalem Temple is preposterous. It's a ruse perpetrated upon the world's population for nearly a thousand years.

How can people know Jesus is divine? Yet, it's true no country has declared war. Scientists have not explained why the lion and the lamb aren't enemies anymore. Or why a river flows from the Jerusalem Temple down to Cairo, Egypt, producing a fertile of bank that grows trees with healing fruits and seeds. Christians claim it rains glory.

Don is adamant that Dr. Stanley Morose has hit upon an idea that will counter fear that the world will soon be destroyed by fire. That the ungodly will be judged then sentenced to an eternal Hell. Or that Satan, the Antichrist, and False Prophet, and demons will dwell with them.

It is a lie that begs to be disclaimed.

Didn't people think the world would suddenly change when 1999 ended on December 31? Nothing catastrophic happened. Smart people solved the problem. "Just like they will today," Don believes.

# 45

**BECCA FINISHES HER LAST** class for the day at 4 p.m. She stops to purchase a Subway sandwich since she hadn't eaten anything since breakfast. For the past thirty minutes, while driving back to the apartment, she's thought of nothing but Don and how to convince him that the Bible is true. He needs salvation. To be safe from harm.

She tosses her handbag on the sofa and places her file case on the floor beside her desk and sighs. Maybe the best way to help Don understand the power of Jesus is to encourage him to read what happened to one of her ancestors in 376 ACR. Mary Ann Simpson.

Becca goes to the bookshelf and locates the diary passed down to her father by his great-grandfather. It contains the story of Mary and her unlikely marriage to Gray Simpson. He was unschooled, a widower who owned a grocery store. Mary was intelligent, well-educated, an astronomer that worked for an observatory in southern Arizona.

But their story is far from ordinary. It's magical.

Becca opens the diary and carefully thumbs through its fragile pages. Mary's story is recorded near the middle. The diary contains many historical facts concerning the genealogy of the Goldman clan. David Goldman was mentioned only once. His story was recorded in another diary by another family member living in another location.

She sits at her desk and rereads the account of Gray and Mary's visit to Jerusalem. They were engaged at the time and planned to marry on Sunday following their visit with King Jesus on Friday during one of the Jewish festivals. No one ever knew what Jesus said to Mary while she was with Jesus in the Holy of Holies at the Temple. But whatever it was left a spiritual glow on her face that required covering.

It was said that few people received that anointed glow—one like Moses had on his face after seeing Jehovah God on a mountain top. The glow was so unusual, people trailed Mary everywhere in Jerusalem the following day, a Saturday. Many attended her wedding ceremony on Sunday. When Gray, the groom, removed Mary's veil and saw her face, he fainted. She closed the diary. Don must hear this story.

Don is home by six p.m. He claims to have a headache and goes straight to the medicine cabinet for something stronger than Tylenol.

Mary debates on whether to resume their morning discussion regarding faith. He's not in a good mood, so she decides to wait telling him about Mary's story recorded in her family's diary.

They eat supper in silence. She wants to ask him what happened during the BBC TV interview with Dr. Morose, but doesn't. He will tell her about it in time. Then she'd show him the diary and tell him what happened to Mary after she visited Jesus at the Jerusalem Temple.

*But will he even listen, much less believe the historical account?*

When they retired to bed, it was very dark and cold outdoors and snowing huge flakes. Tomorrow would make for difficult travel.

* * *

The following day was like any other and time seemed to fly by. For the rest of the week, Don came home late. Though he has a degree in bio-science, he works for a  real estate agency owned by a wealthy Arab, the only son of aristocratic Iranian parents. The company buys and sells internationally, but Don deals mostly with local properties.

The weekend arrives. Becca has prayed all week for the right time to sit Don down and read to him what was written in the old diary about Mary and Gray's experience with King Jesus in Jerusalem.

They watch a football game on television. Don's team doesn't win, so he's not in a favorable mood. Becca pops some corn and serves it to him in the den.  They eat in silence until she can stand it no longer.

"Don, I need to show you something."

He's reading a scientific magazine.

She nudges him on the arm. "It's important."

"What is it?" he asks, eyes still perusing the article.

"Promise you'll hear me out before bolting?"

He lowers the magazine and looks at her.

"Is this about Christianity?"

"Not exactly.  It's a love story."

He smiles and draws Becca to his side. "You are beautiful. Do you know that?  I fell in love with you despite your foolish beliefs."

"And I love you, too, Don.  And respect your views."

"Do you?  Really?"

She nods.  "But some topics need to be discussed."

"You mean our differences when it comes to religion."

He chuckles, but to Becca it isn't funny.

"Okay, okay, Love. Tell me your story."

"Thank you."

Becca retrieves the diary from the bookshelf and opens it to the correct page.  "This is a love story about Gray and Mary Simpson."

"I'm listening."

"They lived in Arizona.  Gray's wife died.  They dated and became engaged. They traveled to Jerusalem in 695 ACR to get married."

Don interrupts. "Is this story about Jesus?"

"You promised to listen," Becca reminds him.

He nods.  *Go ahead.*

"Well, they both wanted an interview with King Jesus."

"I knew it!" Don bolts to his feet.

She touches his hand. "Please.  For me.  Listen."

He shakes his head then sits down.

*Go ahead*, the silence says.

"They planned to be married two days after their visit with Jesus."

Becca reads directly from the diary.

Don seems to grow more interested, an answer to prayer.

When Mary finished reading, Don asked, "Did anyone ever know what Gray saw when he lifted Mary's veil on their wedding day?"

"Not then," she replies. "The rest of this story was not recorded until years later by one of their children. When Mary came out of the Holy of Holies after talking with Jesus, her face was glowing so brightly people shaded their eyes. They were afraid because they'd heard tales about people dying who had viewed the Glory of God."

"And you believe this fantastic story?" Don sighs.

"Yes."

"When Gray removed Mary's veil, what did he see?"

"Well, he didn't die. Listen to what her daughter wrote: *My mother is a special person.  When she married my father, her face was scarred from a housefire. My father loved her because she was beautiful inside. After she visited with Jesus, her face glowed.  When my father took off her veil on their wedding day, her scar was gone. Jesus had healed my mother.  She was absolutely beautiful."*

Don sobers.  "And you believe this, Becca?"

"Why would anyone record such a story in their diary if it wasn't true?" she queries.  "All I'm asking is for you to have an open mind about Jesus.  Read the Bible and learn more about God."

"Will you get off my case then?"

"Don't you want to know the truth?"

"That's not an answer."

"I love you. Isn't that good enough?"

He picks up the empty bowl of popcorn and starts toward the kitchen.  "Don?  This is more important than your job."

He spins around.  "Is Jesus going to pay our bills?"

Becca sighs.  She's tried.  Only God can prompt him now.

# 46

**ANOTHER WEEK PASSES** with busy schedules getting in the way of furthering Becca's conversation with Don concerning biblical truths. Jesus has been chosen by God to bring salvation of souls to Earth. The Jews first, but religious leaders rejected him as the Messiah. So, He extended salvation's invitation to Gentiles through the Apostle Paul's testimony. The Church Age came about so all people could know about God's impartial grace.  But, like yesterday, many do not listen.

It is almost nine p.m. and Becca is already in bed, but the lamp is turned on. She cannot fall asleep until she knows Don is safely home. During the past month, there have been news reports of thefts, carjackings, and muggings. People are desperate to feed their families and pay their bills.  No person is safe on the streets after dark.

It has not rained in Atlanta for over a year. Georgia farmers complain about the drought. Florida's fruit industry has failed. The supply line of materials from other countries are in gridlock at ports.

The weather problem is due to the fact no resident has recently travelled to Jerusalem to pay homage to Jesus. Withholding rain from areas where people reject His kingship fulfills an Old Testament prophecy. Yet, modern society ignores the idea as foolish. They blame bad weather on climate change.  Life will certainly change at the end.

She hears noises downstairs. Someone is in the apartment.

*Is it Don, or a thief?*

"Don't be silly, Becca." She slips out of bed and tiptoes over to the bedroom door to listen for more activity.  None.

*Disturbing, still.*

"Well, better to face the enemy than fear the consequences."

Becca throws on her robe and tramps downstairs barefoot to the foyer. Nothing.  Perhaps, she simply imagined an imposter.

"Ma'am?"

Becca turns around and faces a stranger standing in the living room. He's tall and slender, dressed in a pair of khaki pants with a plaid cotton shirt.  His eyes are a strange color purple and his hair is golden.

"Who are you?" Becca asks.

"I've gone by many names."

Becca thinks about his answer.

"Are you God?"

The stranger chuckles. "No, I'm lesser."

"Why are you here?"

"To deliver an invitation."

"What kind of invitation?" Her heart leaps at the oddness.

"The King has invited you to visit him."

Becca knows of no other person on earth who refers to himself as King. No other monarchies exist in the millennium.

"King Jesus wants to see me?" Becca inquires.

The anonymous visitor nods affirmatively.

"Is it a written invitation, or you just telling me?"

"Verbal. Will you come and bring Donald?"

"You know my husband?"

"I know of him," he replies.

"Don will be home shortly. Maybe you should speak directly with him. He isn't a Christian and he won't come with me."

The stranger smiles, a glow on his cheeks.

"What?" Becca thinks she is missing something.

"Your husband will come, trust me."

"Because you will make him?" The idea is startling.

"No. Because he will run to King Jesus for answers."

Then he simply evaporates into thin air.

Becca sinks to the marble floor, stunned. An angel just came to her door and extended a personal invitation to visit King Jesus. Doesn't that mean that Jesus cares about every lost, wandering soul?

*Even my husband, Don.*

* * *

Morning arrives and Becca discovers she's slept all night on the sofa. The wind rustles in the bushes outside her window. With the curtains drawn, she cannot see dark clouds, but she suspects the day is overcast. She dreads going back upstairs to shower and dress.

Reality sets in. *What time is it?*

She patters into the kitchen and stares at the microwave clock. 8:20 a.m. She'll be late for her university class if she doesn't hurry.

*First, coffee. No day starts right without a shot of caffeine.*

Besides, she needs to locate Don and tell him about her angelic visit. Hopefully, he will see the urgency of accompanying her to Jerusalem to meet with King Jesus. The angel had specifically asked Becca to bring him. *Because he will run to King Jesus for answers.*

She didn't understand when or how that could happen—seeing through a glass darkly as Paul had described the 3$^{rd}$ Heaven.

*But life always presents a surprise.*

Becca makes coffee and has a light breakfast of toast and jam. She showers and hurriedly dresses for the day, determined to find Don as soon as her morning classes end. If he didn't call, she'll find him.

*This is an urgent mission. An invitation to see King Jesus.*

# 47

**DON DID NOT COME** home that day or the next, so Becca became worried. Did he receive a work assignment that suddenly took him out of the country? Is that why he hasn't phoned? What is going on?

When Don had been missing forty-eight hours, Becca decided to go down to his office and quiz his secretary about his whereabouts. Perhaps, he is upset with her for pushing him to study the Bible and needs some space away from home. No, from her. The nagging wife.

*But two days and no word?*

All she'd been trying to do is help Don see the biblical truth that faith through grace is the only way to secure his place in Heaven.

*But he's failed to take Jesus seriously.*

Friday morning, Becca phones the university to tell them she is taking a personal day off. She asks her secretary to post a note on the door of her room instructing students to go online to receive their Monday assignment. That done, she gets in her Buick and drives downtown where Don has his office in a high-rise on $2^{nd}$ Street.

Traffic is horrendous. Drivers of big SUVs are bullish as well as delivery and transport trucks. People wave their hands at her in protest.

*Get out of my way!*

When the end comes, all of this will be gone. Fire will swipe the earth clean, then Jesus will turn all of His authority back over to the Father, who will create a new invincible world for the saved to live.

*Heaven.*

Becca parks in a high-rise garage across the streets from Don's building that houses the real estate agency were he spends most of his time working. She obeys the redlight and waits for the crossing sign.

It's a trip up five stories to reach the floor where she needs off. No one on the elevator pays attention to her. They all look unhappy.

*Where the lion and the lamb find harmony, why can't people?*

She opens the door to the suite and approaches the front desk.

"I'm here to see my husband, Donald Pinson."

"I'll ring his secretary."

Becca waits anxiously. Something doesn't feel right. First, his not coming home. Then the visit from the angel. And now, the third day and no word from him. It's like—she doesn't know. Surreal.

"Julie says she hasn't heard from him since Wednesday."

"What time on Wednesday?" Becca asks.

"Just a minute."

Becca waits while Lorrie relays the question to Julie.

"He left in a hurry around ten a.m. on Wednesday."

"Did he say where he was going?" Becca inquires.

Lorie appears frustrated. "Why don't you and Julie have this conversation? I have calls coming in that I need to take."

"Sure." That suits Becca just fine.

The door to the hallway is locked, but Lorie opens it for Becca. Don's office is the last one on the right. The door stands open, and she spies Julie seated at her desk going through file folders.

"Oh, hi, Becca. What's all this about Don?"

Becca drops her purse on the side sofa as she sits.

"You tell me. He hasn't been home in three days."

Julie gets up and closes the door.

The act somehow upsets Becca.

"Has something happened to my husband?"

Julie resumes her position at the desk. Her eyelids are droopy over a set of dark gray eyes. "He left in a big hurry on Wednesday."

"Okay . . ." Becca pauses. "Was he sick?"

"I don't know. Don had an appointment with a representative from an oil-company executive at 9:30 a.m.," Julie reveals, tilting her head in thought. "Thirty minutes later, he came out of his office and left. No explanation where he was headed. It may be nothing."

"Regardless of where Don went, it isn't like him not to call if he isn't coming home," Becca says. "I'm filing a Missing Person Report."

"Is that wise? Maybe you should give it another day."

"Thank you for your time."

Becca is even more worried about Don. None of this makes any sense. She gets in her Buick and morphs into the Atlanta traffic. It's a short drive down to the Police Station. She fills out the paperwork and speaks with a detective. He promises to look into the matter. But Becca knows that might not be soon enough to help Don.

Knots in her stomach, Becca opts for an early lunch. She pulls into the parking lot at her favorite Chinese restaurant and kills the motor. The maître d' knows her by the first name. She's given their usual seat at a table by the window—hers and Don's.

This is a bad idea. Becca swipes tears from her cheeks. Everything in here reminds her that Don is missing.

Their regular waiter shows up with water and a menu.

"Mister Don?" he inquires with an accent; he's the brother of a brother of the owner who regularly brings in relatives from their homeland, gives them work, and finds them a place to live.

"Have you seen him here recently?" Becca inquires, opening the menu while glancing down so she can hide her tears.

"No Mister Don for lunch since last week," Xi replies.

"I'll have the egg-drop soup with your house salad," she decides.

"Yes M'm." Xi quickly departs to take care of her order.

Through a window, Becca stares at the tall buildings blocking the murky Atlanta skyline. Where is Don? Is he injured and can't call?

Becca finishes her meal and pays her tab with cash. She is back at the apartment by 2:15 p.m. Letting herself in with a key, she startles.

"Donald Pinson! I was worried sick! Where have you been?"

"Were you followed?" He glances into the hallway.

In the next few seconds, Becca feels the tight grip of her husband's hand on her right arm as he catapults her inside the apartment, slams the door and locks it. "Are you sure?"

Becca is breathless. "I wasn't followed."

He breathes a sigh of relief.

Becca switches on some lights to dispel the dismal darkness in the apartment. "What's going on, Don? I feared you'd been kidnapped."

"No, no—" He combs his fingers through his thick dark hair. "It's much more complicated than that, Becca. I'm in serious trouble."

"What's happened?"

Don drags Becca over to the sofa and sits down with her, his hands holding tightly to hers. "I made a huge mistake."

"What kind of mistake?" Becca regrets having gone to the police to report Don missing. It won't be long before a detective shows up at their door to look around the apartment for clues that might tell him where Don went. Only, Don is here. And it will look like she lied.

"I made a mistake too," she quickly adds.

Don appears confused.

"Explain, please."

"No. You, first."

# 48

WE WERE PACKED AND ready to leave before 4 a.m. the following morning. Don had arranged our flight to London, England, departing at 6 a.m. We were going to the airport in an Uber. Incognito.

Becca had listened to Don's explanation as to why a terrorist was looking for him. He'd sold a high-rise building in Stone Mountain to an Arab who appeared impeccably financially qualified since he represented a foreign oil company based in Dubai, Emirates. Don had no idea the downpayment for the building came from a terrorist group.

Anxious to close the deal and receive a huge commission, he'd failed to do his homework and trace the origins of the funds put down. He'd deposited the escrow money in the bank where his company had a commercial account. Only the funds did not land in the right place.

"I lost the escrow money," Don had explained to Becca. "It looks like I stole the money." He'd been sweating by that time.

Becca had asked how he might solve the dilemma.

Don said he'd contacted an FBI friend and asked him to run the Arab purchaser's mug through a facial-recognition program—to confirm the man had no prior arrests. Turns out the Arab's cousin was the current leader of Syria's Ba'ath organization. Don had made a gross error that jeopardized his company and his freedom. When the funds were reported missing, he'd be arrested and jailed. In essence, he had cleaned the money intended to fund a terror organization.

All of this information was swirling through Becca's brain as they exited the Uber at the airport entrance and gone straight to the concord where a Delta Flight was currently boarding. Don offered his phone to verify their tickets and they got on the flight to London.

Becca's thoughts have been so thick all morning she cannot thin them out enough to discern them. But, just like her angelic visitor had predicted, Don had said, "We need to leave the country."

It wasn't Israel, but it was closer. Now they were fugitives from the law. The flight lifts and Becca glares at Don. He's remorseful.

"I'm so sorry, Becca. I'd already anticipated selling the building so I found us a nice house east of Atlanta in Gwinnett County."

"I'm sorry, too, Don. But now that we're leaving America, I have a request." This might be her last chance to convince Don to arrange a visit with Jesus at the Jerusalem Millennial Temple.

"Anywhere you want to go, but after I talk to the person in charge of the CIA London office. Peter called him and arranged a meeting."

"Your friend with the FBI?"

"Yes. Peter was my roommate in college. I trust him with my life."

"You better."

Don grasps Becca's hand. "I need the CIA's help. I'm innocent—but it looks like I am guilty since the down payment is missing."

"All anyone has to do is check our bank account."

"It's not that simple," Don replies as the plane levels off at 42,000 feet above earth's surface. "My account was closed yesterday."

"You closed your account?"

"No, you did, according to the bank manager."

Becca knew she hadn't done it, so who posed as her and closed the account? "Do we have a new account?"

"Probably." Don sighs.

"Where?"

"In the Cayman Islands, or Iran, where U.S. bank snoops can't get to it," Don answers. "Whoever set me up knows what they're doing."

The problem suddenly becomes painfully transparent.

Don holds Becca's hand. "Get some sleep, you'll need it later."

"Wait!" Becca needs answers. "Will the CIA guy believe your story? Am I in trouble, too?" It was her according to the bank that had the credentials to close their bank account and move the funds.

By this time, Don's eyes are closed, his head resting on the back of the seat, and he's slightly snoring. Poor guy. Becca sighs.

* * *

When Don and Becca deplane, it is morning in London. They go through customs unquestioned and take a city cab over to a hotel to check in under an assumed name that Don's FBI friend arranged.

At least one person is on their side.

The meeting with the CIA station manager is not scheduled until later tonight. Saturday. London streets are filled with international visitors here to view a play-off basketball tournament between teams from Mexico and Spain.  Don and Becca fit right in, so they decide to have lunch at a popular restaurant across the street from Hyde Park.

Becca is ravished, so she orders the grilled salmon with fresh-baked veggies.  Don opts for a lobster bisque with a mixed salad.

They eat heartily, drink several cups of coffee, trying to adapt to the time change.  Don pays the tab in cash and they cross the street to the park.  This is a good opportunity for Becca to make her request.

Don's gaze flits in many directions.  She watches him closely.  He's concerned they have been followed. Any Middle-Easterner that walks past becomes a concern. Anyone wearing sunglasses startles him, so they get up and walk around until Don is certain they are not followed.

Becca has seen clandestine movies, but never thought she'd be caught up in a real drama.  Finally, they return to the hotel. Don makes sure the door is locked to their suite then closes all the window curtains.  He's restless and looks weary.  Troubled to the soul level.

"Don?" Becca decides to make her move.

His eyes settle uneasily on her. "I'm so sorry, honey."

"I know you are, Don." She sits on the sofa with him. The television is turned down low; it's on a popular news channel.

"I think you need advice," she begins.

"Yeah, I do."  His sigh is profound.

"I don't think the CIA has the answers."

He huffs, "Then who does?"

"Jesus," Becca replies.  "Talk to the King in charge."

Don scowls. "He's not my Savior."

"Maybe not," Becca counters, "but that is up to you."

"What do you mean?"

"Jesus never forces His will on anybody.  You choose faith first, then you investigate truth, then you decide if you believe in His kingship over the world.  I wasn't always a believer.  I had to search."

Don shakes his head. "I don't have time for Bible study, Becca. I'm keeping my appointment with the CIA liaison tonight."

"Suit yourself, Don.  I'm going to take a nap."

*He will run to Jesus!* Becca recalls the angel saying.

# 49

**"I ONLY TOOK THIS** meeting because Peter asked me to," claims Joanna Reeves, the CIA station chief in Great Britain. She's wearing casual clothes with a heavy windbreaker over them. Her eyes are a sharp mint-green and constantly roam the area for signs of life. A rat skitters across the cluttered floor and startles Don. He actually jumps.

"Par for the city," she comments.

Don offers a handshake but she ignores it.

"I need someone to understand what's happened," he explains.

They are in a vacant building under construction, inside a room on the second floor. Don had to climb the bones of a staircase.

"Okay, I'm listening." Joanna lights a cigarette, inhales, and blows the smoke into the swift wind attacking the city. "Peter says he believes you are innocent—incapable of such a clandestine plot."

*That is no compliment*, Don assesses her remark. "I did everything according to the law," he says, "but it turned out all wrong."

Joanna drops the unfinished butt and stamps out the flame with a boot. "Story of my life." She chuckles. "So, tell me what happened."

Don sits on a rafter, the wind playing havoc with his hair—a little longer than he usually wears it. He's hiding, so he's changing his image like a chameleon. "Mr. Kakarak called me a month ago," he begins.

Joanna listens attentively, making no notes. Peter said she was top of her class at the FBI farm before the CIA drafted her. I.Q. topping out near genius. Yet, she looks as ordinary as a young school girl. She has to be in her late twenties, but could pass for eighteen.

"So, you deposited the money in your company's special account for earnest money, the down payment on the building, but the funds went elsewhere." Lightning suddenly splits the atmosphere followed by a loud crash of thunder then a downpour of drenching rain. The scant roof overhead does little to stave off the chaotic weather.

"We need to get to shelter," Joanna says, already walking.

They end up in a small bistro in the heart of a rundown part of London where they order coffees. Don suspects the station manager has snoops here working for the CIA. All this clandestine stuff is unfamiliar and scary to Don. He's always been a straight shooter, never aiming at anything illegal. He isn't rich, but has made enough selling properties to save more than he pays out. He wants a home, a family, and the safety of knowing nobody is going to kill him.

"Look," Joanna says with finality, "I'll have someone trace the money and see where it went. I'll call you." She hands him a burner.

"You believe me." Don feels a little better about the situation.

"Never call me again on the number Peter gave you."

Don nods. He's grateful, will not dictate any demands.

* * *

He is back at the hotel a few minutes after midnight. Today is Sunday. Becca usually attends church while he fine-reads the financial reports from the prior week. This day will prove entirely different.

"Where were you, Don?" Becca lifts her head from the pillow as he slides under the bedcovers beside her. "I was worried."

"I met with the station chief—she's a woman. Young, but smart," he explains. "Said she'd get someone to trace the earnest money on the sale and see where it went." He yawns. "Then I just walked."

"In the rain? In the dark? Are you insane?"

By this time, Becca is fully awake. "Don, someone's after you. Please don't take any unnecessary chances. I can't lose you."

He rolls over and embraces her. "We won't, I promise."

"I know you mean well, but you're not God."

He sits up. "Why do you keep bringing Him up?"

Becca slings her legs off the others side of the bed.

"Don, I need to tell you something and it can't wait any longer." She gets out of bed and switches on the ceiling light.

"I'll make us some hot decaf tea and you will listen this time."

Ten minutes later, they are seated at the bar drinking the hot beverage. The warm mug feels good to Don's cold hands. He feels safe here in the hotel, beside Becca, where no one is watching.

"What can't wait any longer?" Don inquires.

"You recall the story about Mary Ann Simpson's visit with Jesus?" she asks. "How the scar on her face was healed after seeing Him?"

"I do. What's any of that got to do with my situation?"

"Just this—you need a miracle to get out of this terrible situation. I know if you ask King Jesus to help you, He will."

"How do you know that?"

"An angel came to the apartment and invited us to visit Jesus."

"An angel.  Do you know how ridiculous this sounds, Becca?"

"Not to me.  He said you'd leave the country, and you did. He said you'd run to Jesus, so you will.  I just don't know when or how."

# 50

**LONDON IS MASKED IN** a thick fog when Monday arrives. Don slept while Becca prayed the rest of the night.  Surely, if an angel came to invite them to Jerusalem, Don would go. She was up early and made coffee. Their hotel suite has a small kitchen with a microwave and toaster oven, which makes it convenient to prepare quick meals.

Becca can tell Don has lost weight since Wednesday, so she nukes bacon in the microwave and makes cinnamon toast. Don will be pleased. She glances up as he stumbles into the kitchen and plops down on a barstool.  Without asking, Becca pours him a mug of black coffee.

"I made you breakfast."

"I'm a bit nauseated."  He sips on the strong java.

"Putting something on your stomach will help, Don."

Becca hands him a plate with the bacon and toast.

"Please eat something, Don.  You've lost weight."

"I was a bit chubby in the stomach anyhow."  He recalls he hasn't eaten since lunch yesterday.  The food smells good so he digs in.

Becca watches her husband devour the food and ask for more. This pleases her greatly.  But all is not perfect when she hears a knock at their hotel.  "Are you expecting anyone?" she inquires.

"No.  Maybe it's the station chief with some news."

Don steps across the room and opens the door.  Two men wearing police uniforms stand there.  "Are you Donald Pinson?"

"Yes."

"Come with us to the station.  Our Chief has questions."

Don glances back at Becca.  Horror is written into her expression.

"I'll get my coat."

No use resisting arrest. This might be just an interrogation session to exonerate him from the accusations that he stole the earnest money the buyer put down on the sale of a building?  Perhaps, Joanna Reeves will be at the station with the information needed to free him.

"Should I go with you?" Becca helps Don into his jacket.

One officer hands her a business card.  "We'll phone."

She nods. The situation is out of their hands. It's up to the angel to intervene. Somehow, she knows everything will work out in their favor. It's a matter of faith in the One Who controls everything.

* * *

When Don arrives at the police station he is placed in an interrogation room. Station Manager Joanna is not there. This upsets Don since she's promised to locate the lost earnest money. What kind of defense does he have now? How did the police locate him?

A tall man that resembles a skeleton walks into the interrogation room and stands at the end of the table, across from Don. His face is sallow—a sign of liver disfunction. And he appears to be in his seventies. He slaps a folder on the table and drops in a chair.

"Who are you?" Don inquires.

"Your worst nightmare."

"I want an attorney."

"You sure? What if I want to cut a deal with you? Let you walk. That is, if you cooperate with us," the thin man says.

"I didn't steal any money," Don defends himself.

Tall and thin opens a folder and slaps it with a withered hand. "The report here says you were the last person to touch a million dollars put down on a commercial property in Atlanta, Georgia."

Don cannot deny he probably was.

"Care to comment?"

"I did everything according to the book," Don claims. "I deposited the money in our company's escrow account."

"No physical evidence you did," Tall and Thin remarks.

Don inhales deeply, thinks about a response.

"I want an attorney. Right now!" He sits back.

"Suit yourself." The interrogator leaves the room.

Next thing Don knows, the two officers that brought him to the station are escorting him down a long, drab hallway to lockup.

So much for seeing a lawyer today.

* * *

When Don doesn't phone, Becca starts to worry even more. What about his one call? Did it go to an attorney? Does the American law apply here in Great Britain? She finds the card the police officer handed her and dials the number.  It's busy.  She tries again. Still busy. After ten times, she gives up and locates her Bible.  This is a matter for Jesus to solve.  Or the angel who came to visit her a few days ago.

A Psalm written by David soothes Becca.  *Psalm 119: 161.* She begins reading. *"Princes have persecuted me without cause, but my heart fears only Your word.  I rejoice over Your promise like one who finds vast treasure. I hate and abhor falsehood, but I love Your instruction. I praise you seven times a day for your righteous judgments."* She closes the Bible and prays.

# 51

**DURING THE COLD DARK** night in lockup at the London Police Station, Don thinks about what Becca told him. Jesus performs miracles. He never imagined he would need one since he always obeyed the law. His parents taught him right from wrong. But it appeared none of that mattered now. The evidence—though false as far as he was concerned—is what counts. Maybe Becca is right to have faith in a Higher Being. Someone that can stand above circumstances and view every angle of the tangled truth. Don did something he never does, he bowed his head and prayed: *God, if you're real, I need help.*

He must've dozed off without realizing it. Suddenly, there was a presence beside him. The cold cell felt warmer, safer. He opened his eyes. A man with tender eyes the color of eggplant stood there.

"Who are you? My lawyer?"

"More like help in troubled times."

Don actually smiles. "I think someone already wrote that song."

The stranger clears his throat. "Do you want to get out of here?"

Don blinks. If this isn't an attorney, who has the power to release him? "Did you pay my bail?" He wobbles as he stands.

"No need." The stranger points over his shoulder.

Don notices the door to the cell stands open.

"I can just leave?"

"Yes, with me. Like Paul did."

"I don't know anybody by that name." Don isn't going to look a Gift Horse in the mouth and turn him down. "Let's get out of here."

"Great idea!"

They walk down the hallway and out the front door with nobody noticing or stopping them. It makes little sense to Don, but the fresh outdoor air feels like freedom has arrived. "Where to now?"

"Becca's in the car waiting for us," the stranger says.

"Do you have a name?"

"Does it matter? I'm here to help."

"Did God send you?" Don asks as he slips into the backseat of the SUV and taps his sleepy wife on the shoulder. "Hey, honey."

"Hey, Don.  How are you feeling?"

"Much better now that I'm free."

The angel sent by Jesus pulls out into traffic.  They drive straight to Heathrow International and use their boarding passes to get on a plan going to Israel. Don will not question what is taking place.

Becca has arranged for him to talk to King Jesus.

The three of them sit together on the flight.  Oddly, the stranger isn't in the mood to have a conversation, but Becca asks too many questions.  "Look, hon.  You know as much about this as I do."

Finally, she gives up and lays her head back on the seat.  Her lips are barely moving. Don knows she is praying.  He should pray, too.

Five hours, non-stop, the plane lands at a private airport in Tel Aviv.  The three of them get off. Out front, a cab is waiting for them.

Don smiles as he holds Becca's hand.

"This is service, honey."

She smiles back.  "I'm glad you are happy."

"I am."

"Sir?" Becca addresses their escort. "Are you sure we can see King Jesus without going through all the training required?"

"What training?" Don asks, concerned.

"This is a special meeting," the angel answers. "At the request of the King, protocol is skipped. Besides, Don would never get a pass through the road beside the River of Life.  Only the holy walk there."

Don feels confused. "What is he talking about?" he whispers to Becca, worried for the first time.  Is the man calling him a sinner?

"I'm sure everything will be just fine, Don," Becca responds. "Let's just trust our guide and see how it all plays out."

The cab lets them off at the Jerusalem Temple.  Becca brought a change of clothes and toiletries with them, so the cabbie sets the luggage on the concrete walk.  The fare has already been paid.

*Jesus thinks of everything,* Don notes.

It's mid-morning on Tuesday and people are lined up to go inside the temple.  Their angelic guide leads them to the front of the line and they enter through impressive portals to get inside the temple.

Don has never viewed any building so beautiful. There are gold and silver pots filled with live green plants and colorful flowers. The ceiling above them stretches up to the second story. Walking through this spacious room feels like entering a wealthy palace, but ordinary folks mill around as their guides lead them through various rooms.

Don is mesmerized by it all.

*What's going to happen to me?*

"Wait here!" the angel orders.

"Is God in there?" Don points to a door.

"King Jesus is inside. He is God's Son—but they are One." Becca pauses. "I'll explain the Trinity later. Let's just go with the flow."

Don's brain is skittering. The flow is faster than his brain.

The angel comes out the door and looks at Don.

"The King will see you now."

Don walks through the door and enters Fairy Land. There is light and peace and hope and love—all rolled into one in this part of the temple. He feels his knees bend and goes with the flow as he kneels before Jesus. The King's magnificent eyes sparkle like the stars of universe. The door is closed and they are alone. Don is afraid to speak. What if he says the wrong thing? So, he waits and waits and waits.

Finally, Jesus says, "I hear you are in trouble."

"How do you know that?"

"Your wife. She prays for you."

"I know she believes in you," Don says.

"But prayers go back way longer than that for you."

"What do you mean?" Don asks.

"Your great grandfather. Zach, short for Zachariah. He was Jewish, did you know that?" King Jesus falls silent.

Finally, Don answers, "I guess I did, but I never thought much about it," he admits. No use lying to—."

Jesus smiles. "I know faith is new to you."

Don is embarrassed. What did I say wrong?

"I am Alpha and Omega, the Beginning and the End."

Don nods. "You read my thoughts."

Jesus nods.

"So, my great-grandfather, Zach, prayed for me?"

"Yes, Don. He asked me to bless his offspring to the third and fourth generation. Only your grandfather failed to believe the Torah and trust that I am the Messiah sent by God.  So, the blessing was delayed." Jesus pauses, waiting for Don to perceive the meaning.

"Okay, I get it," Don says.  "And that is why I am here—because my wife and great-grandfather prayed for you to bless me."

"Exactly, Donald.  So here is your blessing."

Still on his knees, Jesus approaches Don and lays his hand on his head.  "I call you as one of mine.  You are forgiven of your sins and welcomed into the Kingdom of God.  Trust in the Lord with your whole heart, and lean not to your own understanding."

Don opens his eyes, dripping with tears.

"That sounded like a scripture of sorts."

"It is." Jesus smiles.

When the room is silent, Don stands up.

"Should I go now?"

"Do you have any questions?"

"I kinda like to know why you appear as a man."

Jesus laughs.  "That troubles a lot of people."

"You can be anything, right?"

"In my glory state, I am pure energy.  God, the Father, is spirit as well as His Helper, the Holy Spirit.  I was sent to earth to rectify some wrongs created by Adam and Eve.  Their sin of disobedience."

Don listens intently, trying to comprehend the idea.

"If I look like you, think and speak like you, doesn't that help you understand Who I am? The prayers of the saints help Us understand what you are going through on earth." Jesus inhales deeply.

"That's a lot to take in, Jesus," Don admits.

"It takes faith, my child.  And searching."

"Yes, it does," Don agrees.

"I guess I should go and give Becca an opportunity to speak with you.  She's been begging me to come here for quite a while."

"Yes, go now.  Trust me. All will be fine."

"I'm not in trouble anymore?"

"You are, but I am with you from now on."

Don leaves the Holy of Holies, stunned. Becca anxiously looks at him as he walks past her and out of the Temple into the courtyard.

# 52

## Atlanta, Georgia

**"THE PRISONER CAN'T JUST** walk out of jail without help!" the sheriff screams at the officer in charge last night.

"I swear his cell door was locked," the officer replies. "Nobody came past me—that I could see. Am I in trouble?" Obviously, someone opened the door. It looked like he hadn't done his job.

"Maybe you dozed off," Sheriff Adams says, calming a bit. "That would explain how someone slipped past you."

"Nope. I was wide awake. Three cups of strong straight-up Starbucks my wife fixed for me in my thermos. I saw no one."

The sheriff throws a hand. "Get out of here, George. I'll let you know how this situation shakes out."

"Am I going to lose my job?"

"Undetermined. If we find Donald Pinson, I'll give you a pass this time." The sheriff curses. "Never let a prisoner go again!"

Sam scoots out of the sheriff's office, grateful he still has a job. He saw the cell where the prisoner was in. The door stood open.

The sheriff issued an arrest warrant for Donald Pinson with his picture online. The APB went out nationally to all police stations.

* * *

Becca kneels before King Jesus then sits down on the wooden bench in front of Him. Jesus takes her hands. "Bless you, my child. You have been faithful in much, always prayerful for the needs of others. That touches the heart of God. How can I help you?"

She removes a diary from her large purse.

"I have questions regarding an ancestor of mine. David Goldman. He lived during the 2$^{nd}$ century. According to his son's diary, David left his village in Brazil when Joseph turned eighteen. David said he was returning to Jerusalem. What happened to him?"

"Aren't you interested in his wife, Diana?"

"The prostitute? She died giving childbirth to Joseph." Becca is surprised by the question. "I presume she's buried in Israel."

Jesus smiles. "You presume wrong."

"What do you mean?" Becca sits up straight.

"Four days after she died, I raised her from the grave. David believed she was buried in a public cemetery in Tel Aviv."

"And she never contacted David after her resurrection?"

"No. She believed he loved Dahlia. She let him go."

Becca thinks about the situation. "If You planned to raise Diana from the grave, why didn't you tell David before he left Israel?"

"David was still in love with Dahlia," Jesus explains. "He needed time to settle in his mind that Dahlia was married to his best friend, Milo. By then, David's father had died. David stayed in Bethel and raised Samantha, Thor's daughter. After Joseph turned eighteen, and Sam had married, he decided to return to Israel. David came to see me and I explained the situation. Diana waited for him to return."

"She never remarried in all those years?"

"I know the future, Becca. I asked her to wait for David."

She inhaled deeply.

"It's a sweet love story. David saved Diana from a life of prostitution, but she saved him when he returned to Tel Aviv. They started a business. David became famous for his religious artifacts."

"Wow!' Becca exclaims. "I never would have guessed all that."

"You see, dear, I have a plan for every person born on earth. The faith and prayers of the saints reach Heaven, and their steps are ordered according to the working of the Holy Spirit indwelling them."

Becca inhales the sweet odor permeating the room.

"Is the Holy Spirit here now?"

"Yes. He is wind and fire and a quiet presence."

"Will my husband Don be okay?"

"Depends on how he thinks of me."

"Whether you are in charge of everything," she says.

"I'm waiting to see if he accepts repentance."

"Then you will grant him freedom from all harm?"

"I didn't promise him that."

Becca left the temple and took a cab over to the hotel where they had a reserved room, compliments of the angelic guide that brought them safely to Jerusalem. Don wasn't there, and that worried her.

* * *

It is already dark in Jerusalem when Don stumbles into a bistro to purchase food and drink.  He is famished from thinking.  He'd sat on a park bench for hours replaying his conversation with Jesus.

The King never said he was not in trouble, but rather that it would all work out.  If the real thief who stole the earnest money is not found, it will appear he is guilty.  The word "faith" keeps surfacing in Don's thoughts.  Jesus said it takes faith to enter the Kingdom of Heaven.

Don has a glass of tea and a ham sandwich then returns to the streets of Jerusalem, just wandering and thinking.  "Dear God, I don't know you, but I want to.  People say I am a sinner.  No, Becca thinks that because I haven't repented of my sins and trusted in Jesus."

*But I haven't done anything wrong*, Don thinks.

By midnight, he is exhausted from walking and thinking.  He's about to pass out from dehydration when the guide that brought them to Jerusalem walks up.  "You should go to the hotel and get some rest."

"Who are you really?  An angel?"

"Yes, I serve the King."

"Where is my hotel?"

"I'll walk you there," Galiele says.

"Thank you."

Becca is in the room, wringing her hands as Don opens the door.

"I'm sorry, honey, I needed to be alone and think."

"I was worried sick about you, Don.  You could've called."

"How long have you been here?  Did you see Jesus?"

"Yes, and I had a very interesting conversation about one of my ancestors," she explains.  "But first, I want to hear about your day."

# 53

## A Week Later

**DON WAS ARRESTED** at the airport the third day following his visit with King Jesus in Jerusalem, Becca recalls as she is walking down a drab hallway to an interrogation room where she will visit him.

Seeing him in leg chains and cuffs does not bring a smile to Becca's lips. He struggles to walk, but manages to reach the metal table between them and drop wearily into a chair. "You have fifteen."

"Thank you, officer," Becca says, relieved to see her husband is still alive and breathing. She'd heard horror stories about criminals behind bars being assaulted by their fellow inmates. And Don is definitely considered a criminal, a flight risk, and the county prison director in charge is taking no chances. Don's famous escape eventually reached reporters and was published online internationally.

In a way, Don was famous—in a negative sort of way.

Becca leans closer to the table and whispers, "Can they hear us?"

Don looks up at the camera attached from a ceiling post and nods. "There's nothing you can say that I haven't already," he declares.

Becca stresses over that remark, then, "I tried calling the Jerusalem Temple to speak to Galiele, but the person answering had never heard of an angel by that name," she explains. "I'm so sorry."

"Sorry doesn't solve my problem." Don frowns.

"I honestly believed Jesus could get you off."

"For a nanosecond, I did, too. But . . ."

"But what?" Becca alerts to news.

"He did say it would all work out," Don explains.

"Like it's supposed to. Like when David Goldman returned to Jerusalem and discovered his wife Diana had been raised from the dead." Becca reaches across the table with a hand, then withdraws it.

*Rules.* She hates them. No touching. No hugging or kissing.

"I know . . ." Don sighs, glancing up at the camera.

"I just wanted you to know I love you, Don.  And that I am expecting our first child in September.  I must have gotten pregnant while we were staying at the hotel in Jerusalem.  I'm glad."

There are tears in Don's eyes.

"Don't worry, I'll bring our son to prison to see you."

He shakes his head.  "I don't want him to grow up thinking I am a criminal, Becca.  I may be imprisoned for the crime of stealing a million dollars from my company, but the guilt lies elsewhere."

"I'm not sure anyone is looking for the real thief," Becca says.

"The insurance company is replacing the money." He nods.

"It's so crazy I want to scream!" Becca admits, a little forcefully.

Don almost touches her hand across the table.  "I know, honey, I know. But I'll be okay, and I'll be out of here in five."

"We don't have five, Don.  The world ends in eleven months."

"Everyone believed that in 1999 and it didn't happen."

"This is different.  Did you accept Jesus as your Savior?"

Don shakes his head no.  "Not yet, but I'm reading the New Testament—the Bible a Gideon layperson gave to me."

"That's great, honey!  You'll see all the things Jesus did when He was here on earth the first time—His promise to the Twelve Disciples to return in the clouds at a future time.  Which is now. Almost a thousand years ago. You'll read where it says the world will be destroyed by fire and Jesus will hand all authority over to the Father. Then they, the Trinity, will create a new, sinless, perfect world where all believers in Jesus will dwell.  Forever and forever and forever."

Don grins.  "It's a nice story, Becca.  A wonderful thought.  I only hope you are right."  The door to the room opens.

"Time to go, Donald."

"My slave driver!  When will you be back?"

"Next month."  Becca watches as Don shuffles out of the room, wondering what plan Jesus has for him.  His situation is unique.

# 54

## Six Months Later

**INTERNATIONAL NEWS MEDIAS** were carefully following what was happening in a Georgia prison located south of Atlanta. It was reported that one inmate had evangelized hundreds of inmates in the past six months. In fact, he'd performed miracle healings and demonstrated an extraordinary understanding of biblical scriptures. Some were calling him a modern "Paul of Tarsus." Readers lapped up the news and called into local stations to ask how they could be saved.

Naysayers who claimed Jesus was a false prophet had tried to stop Donald Pinson and failed. Plots to murder him seemed fated to fail. Even news editors had to admit that Pinson was under the protection of a divine force. Many atheists were beginning to change their minds and trust God's Word, the Bible, that the world was nearing end.

Each month Becca came to visit Don she noticed a difference in him. He was more joyful, content, and could not stop talking about all the inmates who had asked for forgiveness of sin and been baptized by water emersion inside the prison. "Oh, Don, I do miss you!"

"I know you do, Becca." He held her hands. Life had changed for him. The prison guards ignored the rules and gave him special privileges when no one in the main office was looking. "But I've come to understand what Jesus meant when He said it would turn out okay."

"He has called you to a Christian ministry." Becca nods.

"Yes, and people outside the prison are getting saved, too. Atlanta's local newspaper reports that the greatest harvest of souls for Jesus is taking place on the planet. Even terrorists are laying down their weapons peacefully and going back to their homes. I could not have planned a better life, Becca. I trust Jesus and He trusts me."

"That's wonderful, Don! Excellent!' She grasped her abdomen.

"The baby moved?" He smiled. "Are we having a son?"

"Yes, Donald Junior, if that's okay with you."

"As long as Jesus calls him, I'm fine with that name."

Becca glares at her husband.  She never dreamed that their lives would turn out like they had.  "A movie producer has contacted me, Don.  He wants your life story to play out on the big screen."

"Sure.  Has he already interviewed you?"

"I was waiting for your okay," Becca replies.

"Tell him to come and see me soon.  Time is running out."

# 55

## A Week Before the End

**BECCA WAS AT THE** prison by 2 a.m. to visit with Don. He'd been sick for the past two weeks. One prison guard thought he'd been poisoned. He wasn't doing well. Still, he stumbled into the visitation room and sat down at the metal table opposite her.

"I know I look terrible, but I'm okay. Really."

"If you say so." She is unconvinced. "Have you seen a doctor?"

"Several. My organs are slowly shutting down, failing to function."

He coughs, his complexion is sallow; around his eyes, haunted.

"You know, Becca, I never expected to die young, but the idea doesn't bother me anymore," he admits. "Jesus will give me a heavenly body when I rise again." He coughs again. Blood dribbles from his lips.

Becca sucks in a breath to keep from screaming.

"You don't deserve this, honey. You've helped so many people."

"You know how this ends, Becca. Satan and his minions will be released and fight a war against King Jesus in Jerusalem. Nobody who believes in God's authority over the universe understands why Jesus puts up with this rebellion, but I suspect He has a good reason."

"That is faith, Don. More faith than I have."

He grabs her hand. "Don't sell yourself short, honey. You brought me to Jesus through your prayers." His eyes are leaking tears.

"Alongside your Great Grandfather Zachariah's prayers," Becca reminds him. "Jesus told me about that conversation. How the prayers of the saints reach the Father's ears like a sweet aroma. Paul of Tarsus in the New Testament had some comments regarding the subject."

Don nods, chokes up. "If you don't see me again before the final war is over, we'll meet in the Afterlife. I'll be fine, trust me."

Becca laughs. "I do. And I trust Jesus more. We know how this all ends, so we don't have to worry. We are in God's plan. He has His hand in everything that happens to us. Our son will be fine, too."

"They wouldn't let you bring him to see me." Don nods.

"No." She removes some pictures from her pocket. "But the guard said I could show these to you." She hands them over.

* * *

Don passed the next day. He was buried in a public cemetery. While grieving his death, Becca spent her time caring for their son and praying for the salvation of others. Two weeks went by. The thousand-year reign of Christ had reached its conclusion. God was about to make a statement. The Day of the Lord was loud with lightning, thunder, and hard rain. The earth itself was crying out, rebelling as it shuttered.

The Final Battle between good and evil took place on Earth with a deathly grip on humanity. Many people died as nuclear bombs exploded over cities. Polluted air spread over the planet. The angry sun seemed to watch the activity as it heated up exponentially. Scientists reported the star was emitting so much heat so fast that it would soon explode. All communications crashed as satellites burned to a crisp in the atmosphere and soared like shooting stars to the ground.

The war between Jesus and Satan was furious. Becca did not feel the final explosion that wiped vegetation from the surface of the earth then sent the planet hurling aimlessly into space. Her gaze was on Donald, waiting for her, smiling as she moved closer and closer.

Soon, God would hold His Great White Throne Judgment and punish those not marked by the Holy Spirit. They would be judged for their sins and incarcerated forever in a burning Hell with Satan, the Antichrist, and False Prophet. Eventually, God would create a new heavens and earth. A dwelling place for redeemed souls. Heaven.

*The End has come, or is it the Beginning?*

# About the Author

M. Sue Alexander is the author of two Christian-fiction series: *Resurrection Dawn 2014* and *Time of Jacob's Trouble*. Both storylines lead up to a biblical event called The Millennium. During Christ's thousand-year reign on earth, He justly rules from the Jerusalem Temple.

Sue also penned and published a four-book series for general audiences: *Crystal Creek Mysteries*, featuring a widow struggling with aging and all the physical complications that come with it. View her independent books on her website: www.msuealexanderbooks.com

M. Sue graduated from Central High School in Bolivar, TN; earned a Bachelor of Science from Union University in Jackson, TN, and a Masters of Administration from Memphis State University in 1968. She's taught public-school junior-high students, sold residential real estate in three states, and self-published all her books. Sue resides on a farm in Middle Tennessee with her husband and enjoys entertaining.